THE BALLROOM IN SAINT PATRICK'S CATHEDRAL

Louis Phillips

BROADWAY PLAY PUBLISHING INC
New York
www.broadwayplaypublishing.com
info@broadwayplaypublishing.com

First printing: June 2014
I S B N: 978-0-88145-598-4

Book design: Marie Donovan
Page make-up: Adobe Indesign
Typeface: Palatino
Printed and bound in the U S A

THE BALLROOM IN SAINT PATRICK'S
CATHEDRAL opened at the Colonnades Theatre Lab
in N Y C on 2 December 1978. The cast and creative
contributors were:

YANNIS PANYOTOUPOULOS	Stephen Casko
EUNICE PANYOTOUPOULOS	Jacqueline Cassel
NIKOS PANYOTOUPOULOS	Louis Giambolvo
PHILIP PANYOTOUPOULOS	Brady Rifkin
GEORGE JANETAKIS	Bill Noone
PENDAKIS JANETAKIS	Charlie Stavola
TAKIS JANETAKIS	Edward Edwards
ELAINE JANETAKIS	Marcia Hyde
MAX ABRAHAMSON	Nesbitt Blaisdell
MRS SATO	Berit Lagerwall
NURSE	Debra Monk
RITA FOSCOLO	Karen Shallo
HOSPITAL GUARD	Tom Tammi
SAILOR	Peter Scolari
PRIEST	Tom Tammi
HILLMAN O'CLAIR	Peter Kingsley
MRS HILLIARD	Debra Monk
PERSON IN THE WAITING ROOM	Tony Simotes
CAPTAIN HARRISON	Peter Kingsley
Director	Michael Lessac
Lighting design	Randy Becker
Set design	Maura Smolover
Music & sound	Michael Jay
Costumes	Rebecca Kreinem & Tere Elgar
Stage manager	Arthur J Schwartz

CHARACTERS & SETTING

YANNIS PANAYOTOPOULOS, *age 10*
EUNICE PANAYOTOPOULOS, *mother of* PHILIP *and* YANNIS
NIKOS PANAYOTOPOULOS, *husband to* EUNICE
PHILIP PANAYOTOPOULOS, *age 12*
GEORGE JANETAKIS
PENDAKIS JANETAKIS
TAKIS (CHARLIE) JANETAKIS
ELAINE JANETAKIS, *wife to* GEORGE
MAX ABRAHAMSON
MRS SATO
NURSE
RITA FOSCOLO
HOSPITAL GUARD
PRIEST *(can be played by same actor who plays* HOSPITAL GUARD*)*
SAILOR *(can be played by same actor who plays* HOSPITAL GUARD*)*
MRS. HILLIARD, *woman at grave site*
HILLMAN O'CLAIR
PERSON IN THE WAITING ROOM
CAPTAIN HARRISON

(10 men, 2 boys, 5 women)

Time: Late August, 1945

Place: A small town in Massachusetts

For
My Parents
&
The Greek Side of the Family

ACT ONE

Scene 1

(*A small town in Massachusetts. Late August, 1945.
Hospital sounds, then nothing. As the light comes up,
we see, on a raised platform, a hospital bed. In the bed is
YANNIS PANAYOTOPOULOS, a ten year old boy in a white
hospital gown. He carries a plastic identification bracelet
strapped about his left wrist. YANNIS' mother—EUNICE
PANAYOTOPOULOS is with him.*)

YANNIS: Momma, Momma…

EUNICE: I'm here, darling.

YANNIS: Water…water…Momma.

EUNICE: Everything's going to be alright..don't worry,
Yanni… She's getting the water.

(*EUNICE clutches at YANNIS, cradling him awkwardly until
he breaks from her grasp. She seizes him again, attempting
to calm him, trying to keep her son from ramming his head
against the bed's metal frame-work.*)

EUNICE: Don't worry…Mommy's here.

(*While YANNIS is screaming for water, a NURSE appears out
of the shadows. She carries a tray of food.*)

NURSE: I've got some water here.

EUNICE: Yanni, can you hear me? The nurse has
brought the water… (*To the* NURSE) He's delirious.

(The NURSE *attends to* YANNIS.*)*

NURSE: He looks as if he's coming out of it.

EUNICE: Where did you get this water?

NURSE: I got it as quick as I could.

EUNICE: You got it from the tap, didn't you? He's allergic to tap water... Don't you know that? Don't you know anything by now?

(In anger, EUNICE *throws the water across the room. The* NURSE *begins to strap* YANNIS *to the bed.)*

NURSE: He's got to be strapped in.

EUNICE: *(Preventing the* NURSE*)* No straps! ...No straps!

*(*YANNIS *screams wildly in much pain.)*

YANNIS: Momma!

NURSE: I'll get the doctor.

*(*NURSE *runs out.)*

EUNICE: *(Calling after her)* You do that! You want to kill my son? Is that what you want to do? Is that what everybody in this hospital wants to do? *(She turns to her son and holds him.)* It's okay, Yanni...don't worry, darling...don't fight me, Yanni...I'm trying to help you...Mamma's here...Everybody's going to be alright.

Scene 2

(Sirens in the distance. Music. Lights slowly cross fade to that section of the stage used to indicate a small backroom in PENDAKIS JANETAKIS*'s restaurant—The Chicken Coop. This backroom is set simply: A small wooden table, a few chairs, a radio of the period, a few cups and saucers, perhaps a counter. During the montage, the brothers enter one by one and take their positions around the table and the radio. The three Greek brothers are members of the* JANETAKIS *family*

and are all brothers to EUNICE, *whom we have glimpsed
briefly in the previous scene.* EUNICE *is a tall, slender,
black-haired woman of thirty-seven.* GEORGE JANETAKIS
*is the eldest member of the family group. He is a giant of a
man, and when he stands up, he towers over the others. His
black hair is close-cropped, and he is dressed quite casually.
He has worn a coat and tie on only two or three occasions
in his life. Right now he is repairing a small toaster that
has gone on the blink... Seated at the table are* PENDAKIS
and TAKIS JANETAKIS. PENDAKIS JANETAKIS *is about four
of five years younger than* GEORGE, *and he is a "spiffy"
dresser. He wears a cream-colored suit, two-toned shoes, and
he is carefully going over the accounts for the restaurant.
He is the politician of the family and the entrepreneur.
His restaurant is one of the more popular restaurants in
Wamesit—at least the Chicken Coop was popular when it
first opened and had people standing in line to get in. But
now, in 1945, with the sighting of peace on the horizon, and
the desire of people to stay at home and save their money, the
restaurant business has fallen off sharply... The youngest
brother is* TAKIS [Charlie] JANETAKIS, *who is dressed in
his army uniform [P F C] and who studies a racing form.
He is in his late twenties, and when the war is officially
over he will either hang around* PENDAKIS' *Restaurant
or he will go into the used-car business. He wears rimless
spectacles, and already his hair is beginning to thin. He
is the only one of the brothers who has not married... The
brother-in-law is* NIKOS (Nicky) PANAYOTOPOULOS. *He
has been married to* EUNICE *for about fifteen years and he
is always seen smoking a cigar, which he jabs into the air
when he is scoring important rhetorical points. He wears
a loud, almost-Hawaiian sports shirt and trousers that are
a bit too baggy for him. His features are sharp, and he is
greatly animated. He very rarely sits still. He usually makes
his brothers-in-law laugh, for which they hold him in great
affection.)*

VOICE OF JOHN FOSTER DULLES: "At San Francisco, the emphasis was shifted. The charter was substantially rewritten to make the organization one which would promote justice and human welfare. There was a tremendous development of what our commission has referred to as the curative and creative processes. The result will be an organization which is subjected to principles of justice and international law and which is designed to recommend the change of any conditions which might impair those principles or the general welfare or friendly relations among nations...I can see no reasonable ground for Christian people now to hesitate in their support of the San Francisco charter."

(GEORGE *switches off the radio.*)

GEORGE: Two Greeks, three opinions, and they're talking about a United Nations.

PENDAKIS: *(Eating chicken, drinking wine)* Ask Woodrow Wilson. He wanted one and look where the hell it got him.

NIKOS: Made the world safe for Democracy, didn't he? Look how safe the world is now. It's so safe they're blowing everyone up.

GEORGE: They say there's nothing new under the sun.

PENDAKIS: If they make up an organization that keeps people from dying, maybe then I'll listen. Until then it's a lot of hooey.

GEORGE: We better organize this damn restaurant, Pendakis. I need lots of chicken.

TAKIS: Is Max coming or not? I don't have all day.

NIKOS: Listen to him! He doesn't have all day.

GEORGE: Afraid you won't have time to make the Daily Double?

NIKOS: Eisenhower couldn't win the war without him.

TAKIS: I got a heavy date, alright?

NIKOS: Why don't you just send the uniform over! The girl can't be interested in what's inside it.

TAKIS: I look better than you guys ever did.

PENDAKIS: What's wrong with the way I look? I taught you how to dress and don't you forget it.

TAKIS: Well, maybe not you. But look at these guys...

NIKOS: Yeah.

TAKIS: The Yid's twenty minutes late. It's not my fault.

GEORGE: You know what happens? Every time they let Max out of the house, the Synagogue grabs him to make a quorum.

TAKIS: Let him sneak out the back way.

NIKOS: He does. Remember last time? They caught him climbing over the fence. That's the trouble with this city. They've got to make use of every Jew they can get.

TAKIS: It's called a Mazuza.

GEORGE: What the hell is called a Mazuza?

TAKIS: The quorum. They don't call it a quorum. They call it a Mazuza.

NIKOS: How do you know all this? You making it with Max's sister all of a sudden?

TAKIS: I read.

NIKOS: He reads!

TAKIS: That's how I know things. I don't sit around all day listening to this radio with big shots telling me how to run my life.

GEORGE: Since when is John Foster Dulles a big shot?

NIKOS: Don't talk to him. He reads. His idea of a great literary character is Man-of-War.

TAKIS: You're jealous because me and Eunie got all the brains in this family.

NIKOS: Don't start me on this brain talk. Some brains you got. *(To* GEORGE*)* I give him fifty bucks and he bets it on the wrong goddamn horse.

TAKIS: Wait a minute! You said Corregidor.

NIKOS: I said Dead to Rights, you know damn well I said Dead to Rights.

TAKIS: He said Corregidor... *(To* PENDAKIS*)* ...Didn't he say Corregidor?

GEORGE: No. He said Dead to Rights.

TAKIS: Who asked you to butt in?

GEORGE: You did.

TAKIS: I was asking Pendakis.

GEORGE: Charlie, admit you made a mistake.

TAKIS: I don't make five hundred and twenty dollar mistakes.

PENDAKIS: Look, forget the whole thing! It's only money. *(To* NIKOS*)* You want the money? Take the money...

NIKOS: It's not the money...that's not the point...

TAKIS: My own brother-in-law doesn't believe me.

NIKOS: What are you talking about, your own brother-in-law? Your own brothers don't believe you...

TAKIS: *(Takes a ticket out of his wallet)* ...Look there's the fifty dollar win ticket on Corregidor...

NIKOS: *(Shouting in disgust)* What do you want me to do? Frame it?

PENDAKIS: *(Wanting to change the topic)* ...I think I'll tell a great joke! The joke about the Ballroom in Saint Patrick's Cathedral.

NIKOS: I heard it already. I heard it. I heard it.

GEORGE: I think he's heard it.

NIKOS: I never should have married into this family on a bet... A bunch of loonies is what I got, especially that sister of yours sitting around the house all day reciting poetry...

GEORGE: Nicky, let the man tell the story.

NIKOS: I'm the one who told it to him...for Christ sakes... Can't I hear anything around here that I haven't told you guys already?

PENDAKIS: Tell the joke.

NIKOS: You tell the joke.

PENDAKIS: Go ahead.

NIKOS: Tell the joke!

PENDAKIS: You're always making such a big deal of it...

NIKOS: Tell the joke!!

PENDAKIS: This guy goes into May's department store to buy some underwear, but he gets home, he knows right away he's made a mistake. He didn't get the right size, it's cut wrong, it's designed wrong. Every time the poor guy sits down... Well, he's in such great pain, he can hardly sit down.

NIKOS: His voice goes up an octave.

PENDAKIS: What?

NIKOS: His voice goes up an octave.

PENDAKIS: *Skamos!!*...and so the poor guy gets up the next day and walks all the way back to the department store because he's going to exchange it, but this time a saleslady insists on waiting on him, and this poor guy is so shy, he can hardly bring himself to look the lady in the face... *(To* TAKIS*)* Like you, Charlie...I mean he can't bring himself to say outright just what the problem with the underwear is, and she keeps asking him, why you want to exchange it, for, and so finally the guy begins to tell her, "Well, Miss, there was nothing wrong with the underwear until my wife and I went dancing in the ballroom in Saint Patrick's Cathedral." The saleslady hears this and thinks the guy is crazy. "There is no ballroom in Saint Patrick's Cathedral." "That's right lady, and that's just what's wrong with these shorts. There's no ballroom in them either."

(No response)

PENDAKIS: Huh? What the hell's the matter, you stupid? Don't you get it? There's no ballroom in Saint Patrick's Cathedral.

TAKIS: I know.

PENDAKIS: He knows.

NIKOS: He knows. He reads.

PENDAKIS: Sometimes you guys give me a pain.

GEORGE: *(To* PENDAKIS*)* You sure got a way with words, Pendakis.

NIKOS: Pendakis, tell it to Max, and when you got him doubled over with laughter, we'll grab his arm and scratch his signature all over the mortgage. that means the brains here will have to find himself a real job.

TAKIS: Don't worry about me, when I get out of the army, I'll support myself. I've got lots of ideas.

NIKOS: Lots of ideas, huh? Name two.

GEORGE: Name one.

TAKIS: Forget it… You want to know an idea? I'll give you one. I'm gonna change my last name because I'm not gonna get ahead with a last name people can't pronounce most of the time.

PENDAKIS: A lot of good that's going to do you.

GEORGE: You know Louis Haralampoppoulas, the butcher? He changed his last name to Jones, and now he's got to change it back…you know why…because none of his Greek customers can pronounce…

GEORGE, NIKOS, PENDAKIS: *(In unison)* Jones…

TAKIS: Well, not everybody in this world is Greek.

NIKOS: Try Abrahamson and see how far that gets you.

PENDAKIS: *(To* TAKIS*)* Hey, General, get Max to buy the restaurant and we'll all have enough money to get ahead.

NIKOS: I don't care how much money we get. It ain't going to make a dent in the goddamn hospital bills.

PENDAKIS: I don't care how much it costs, Yannis is going to get well, alright? Whatever Yannis wants, he'll get. You want my arm? You can have it up to there. *(Indicates his shoulder)*

NIKOS: I don't want your goddamn arm. I want to know why it has to happen to me. Why do I have a kid who's allergic to everything? You know what they're doing to him now? They're putting cockroaches in his arm. They're injecting him with cockroaches, because there's roach dust in the air, and he's even allergic to the air he breathes. Sell the goddamn restaurant. Who cares? I want to get out of everything.

GEORGE: I told you. If we didn't go into the black market, we weren't going to make it in the restaurant business.

PENDAKIS: Tell them to stick it, George. Men are dying over there and people are getting rich off them.

GEORGE: Oh, what the hell do you expect, Pendakis?

TAKIS: The world stinks.

NIKOS: There goes The Brain talking.

PENDAKIS: When we first opened this restaurant, didn't we have them standing in line? Three or four hours they were waiting to get in here.

NIKOS: Hey, Pendakis, stick it to Max. Right? With Kosher baked beans, he ought to be able to turn this place over in another twenty or thirty thousand years.

(PENDAKIS *opens a ledger and begins writing out checks to pay some of the bills. He examines a stack of cancelled checks and rubber stamps them on the back.*)

GEORGE: Hey, keep that under your hat... Hey, Pendakis, I came with this good business idea...

PENDAKIS: *Pau....pau...pau...*

GEORGE: You know what we're going to tell Max. We're going to tell him pretty soon everybody is going to be coming back home. There won't be enough room around here to breathe.

NIKOS: What do you want to breathe for? The air is full of roach dust.

TAKIS: Where the hell is Max anyway... Huh...

GEORGE: If Max says he is gonna be here, he's gonna be here.

NIKOS: That's right, as soon as he can get out of his...

NIKOS, PENDAKIS GEORGE: *(In unison)* Medusa!!!

TAKIS: *(To* NIKOS*)* ...Okay wise guy, you give me fifty bucks and I'll put it on a sure thing for you...

(Phone rings.)

NIKOS: A sure thing...

GEORGE: Ain't Corregidor running in that race?

TAKIS: I had a hundred dollar win ticket on this one the last time out.

NIKOS: Every time I turn around, you're cashing hundred dollar win tickets. Where the hell is all the money?

TAKIS: Books.

PENDAKIS: *(Answering the phone)* ...Chicken Coop. Pendakis here.

GEORGE: That's probably Max on the telephone.

NIKOS: Tell him to get his ass out of the Synagogue and get over here.

PENDAKIS: No, Eunie. We're all here. You want to speak to Nicky?

(NIKOS shakes his head. He indicates he doesn't want to speak to her.)

PENDAKIS: No, Eunie... Okay... Don't you worry about a thing, Eunie. Everything's going to be alright.

(PENDAKIS hangs up and goes for his hat and coat.)

NIKOS: *(Frightened)* What's the matter? Why doesn't she want to talk to me?

PENDAKIS: We got to get to the hospital. It's Philip!

NIKOS: Philip? How can it be Philip?

PENDAKIS: I don't know anything. She didn't say anything. She doesn't know anything. Let's just go to the hospital, huh?

(During the above, MAX ABRAHAMSON has entered. He is in his late fifties, with reddish brown hair and glasses. He wears a light-weight summer coat over a dark suit, and he walks with a slight stiffness because he is bothered by rheumatism. He carries a black umbrella and he wears a yarmulke, for he has just come from the synagogue, where he has been, as usual, the tenth man. The brothers are rushing out.)

TAKIS: Sorry, Max... No time to explain.

PENDAKIS: Max, you watch the restaurant with Claire. *(He sees the opened ledger and the piles of checks.)* Don't worry about a thing, Max. You don't touch a thing, Max. You don't look at anything.

(GEORGE, NIKOS, and TAKIS have left.)

PENDAKIS: *(call off)* Claire, I'm going... *(He exits.)*

MAX: So everybody's going? ...So, alright. I break my neck to get here.

(MAX stops the dial at a George Burns and Gracie Allen radio show that is in progress.)

MAX: Greeks! They're all crazy.

(Lights gradually dim...he chuckles appreciatively. Lights out. End of scene)

Scene 3

(The Wamesit General Hospital. Emergency Room. The waiting area is indicated simply through the use of folding chairs, some long waiting benches. Off to downstage left is a nurse's waiting station where a NURSE reads a romance magazine and plays a small radio. A United States Air force officer—CAPTAIN HARRISON—is dozing on one of the benches. There is one other person in the waiting room—a YOUNG MAN in work clothes. The radio show from the previous scene segues into the speech coming through the nurse's radio. We hear the voice of Harry S Truman.)

VOICEOVER: *(Truman)* I realize the tragic significance of the Atomic Bomb. It's production and its use were not lightly undertaken by this government. But we knew that our enemies were on the search for it. We know how close they were to finding it. And we knew the disaster which could come to this nation, and to all peaceful nations, to all civilizations, if they had found it first... This is why we felt compelled to undertake

the long and uncertain and costly labor of discovery
and production. We won the race of discovery... the
Atomic Bomb is too dangerous be loose in a lawless
world. That is why Great Britain, Canada, and the
United States, who have the secret of its production, do
not intend to reveal that secret until means have been
found to control the bomb so as to protect ourselves
and the rest of the world from the danger of total
destruction. We must constitute ourselves trustees
of this new force-to prevent its misuse, and to turn it
into the channels of service to mankind. It is an awful
responsibility which has come to use. We thank God
that it has come to us, instead of our enemies; and we
pray that He may guide us to use it in His ways and for
His purposes.

(During the final lines, the member of the JANETAKIS *and
Panayatopoulos families explode into the waiting room
area.* EUNICE *and* NIKOS *lead the way. This is the first time
we have seen the husband the wife together, and we realize
that* EUNICE *is taller than her husband, although* NIKOS's
*animated movements, coupled with the sense of humor,
give the impression that he is the center of attention—his
jabbing, explosive movements are in great contrast to the
almost calm acceptance of his wife... There has been an
addition to the clan at this point—*ELAINE JANETAKIS,
GEORGE's *wife, who has been waiting at the hospital with*
EUNICE. *She is also tall, slender, dark-eyed, and although
only a few years younger than her sister-in-law, she appears
to be much younger. Like* NIKOS, *she has a ready sense of
humor, but often times either something in her speech or in
her movements will give the impression that she has been
stealing a drink every once in awhile to help her cope with
her husband, her family, her personal problems. Thus from
time to time, we might see her take a sip from an unlabelled
medicine bottle, then take a mint to sweeten her breath.)*

HOSPITAL LOUD SPEAKER: Doctor Levine, report to parking lot B...Doctor Levine, Parking lot B.

NIKOS: So what in the hell was Philip doing on the roof? We have floors, don't we? Does he ever walk on the floors? No, it's always the roof, the ceiling, a window ledge, the top of some goddamn fence. I've got one son allergic to everything on the ground.

(*At some point that speech we realize that* NIKOS' *brusqueness and his attempts at humor are his ways of holding on, methods of coping with the depths of his own fears, a way of helping his wife to cope.*)

EUNICE: I don't let him go out there.

NIKOS: I didn't say you did, did I? I'm not accusing you.

EUNICE: I don't know what you're accusing me for.

NIKOS: What the hell did I say?

GEORGE: He's not accusing you, Eunice.

NIKOS: Everybody in this family's got wax in their ears.

GEORGE: (*To* EUNICE, *overlapping*) Didn't you hear what he just said?

NIKOS: It's not my fault that Philip doesn't have a brain in his head.

ELAINE: It's the roof's fault. Go blame it on the roof.

TAKIS: (*To* ELAINE) What are you butting in for?

EUNICE: (*Agreeing with* ELAINE) That's right. Tell him to yell at the roof. Not at me.

HOSPITAL LOUD SPEAKER: Will Doctor Collins please report to the Shorn Pavilion?

NIKOS: He was supposed to be in school this summer. Why in the hell wasn't he in school? He's got to make up sixth grade this summer, doesn't he?

EUNICE: How should I know why he wasn't in school. Where do you think I've been all day?

ELAINE: He and the Vernalis boy were playing Captain Marvel or something.

TAKIS: Captain Marvel... That Vernalis boy is a hoodlum. He ought to be locked up.

PENDAKIS: *(Overlapping)* I'm so sick of hearing about supermen.

(The NURSE *has entered from the up-stage area.)*

NURSE: *(To* GEORGE*)* Are you the father?

EUNICE: Nikos!

NIKOS: Where's my boy? Where is he? We're the parents.

NURSE: *(Stumbles over the name)* Are you Mister Panayotopoulos?

NIKOS: She's got wax in her ears too?

GEORGE: *(Crowds the* NURSE*)* We're all his family.

PENDAKIS: Hey, nursey, I'll find the doctor. I know everybody here.

EUNICE: Pendakis, please... *(To* NURSE*)* ...I want to see Philip. Where is he?

NURSE: *(Intimidated by the family)* If you'll just be seated. The doctor said he'll be right down.

EUNICE: Who'll be right down? Philip?

NIKOS: We have another son in this hospital you know. We ought to get some kind of special treatment around here.

NURSE: Two?

*(*EUNICE *sits.)*

NIKOS: If I don't see my boy right now, I'll make matters worse.

NURSE: The doctor's going over the x-rays now. As soon as he's finished, he'll give you a report.

EUNICE: *(To* ELAINE*)* Make Nicky sit down before he gets us all thrown in jail.

TAKIS: Nicky, I'm going to phone the bet in on Corregidor. Alright?

ELAINE: Oh, for God's sake, Takis!

TAKIS: I thought it would take his mind off things. Alright? I thought it would take his mind off things. Why doesn't anyone in this family give me a little credit?

NIKOS: Shoving that goddamn racing form down your throat will take my mind off things...

*(*PENDAKIS *stands up and starts out.)*

NIKOS: *(To* PENDAKIS*)* Where are you going, hot shot, who knows all the doctors around here?

PENDAKIS: *(Returning)* I thought I'd call Zoe. If Philip needs anything, she can bring it down.

NIKOS: How do I know what he needs? Am I a mind reader all of a sudden?

PENDAKIS: I'm not asking you.

NIKOS: If you want a doctor, look in the bar. That's where all the doctors in this slaughter house are.

GEORGE: I don't care what anybody says. We'll just take the elevator up.

*(*GEORGE *crosses to the nurse's station.)*

GEORGE: *(To* NURSE*)* What floor is he on?

NURSE: If you'll just be patient, I'm certain everything is going to be alright.

(We hear ambulance sounds from outside.)

NIKOS: *(To* PENDAKIS*)* Are you going to call Zoe or are you not going to call Zoe?

PENDAKIS: I just want to know what's going on, that's all.

ELAINE: I say get Doctor Ekytis... He's our family doctor.

NIKOS: Ekytis? He's a bum. Get Sarandaris down here. He'll be right down here.

EUNICE: At first report, they said it was a concussion.

NIKOS: What do doctors know? They're only going to pick out something that costs a lot of money anyway.

TAKIS: I think Sarandaris is in Boston.

NIKOS: So what? I'll go to Boston for him.

GEORGE: Hell, no. You guys always go to Boston. This time you stay here.

ELAINE: What? Are you crazy or something? Just call him.

TAKIS: If he wants to rent a plane, tell him I'll send him the money!

PENDAKIS: We'll all send him the money.

NIKOS: Are you going to call Zoe or not? Or do I have to do everything around here myself?

ELAINE: What's wrong with Ekytis? He delivered my three kids, didn't he?

NIKOS: Three good reasons not to call him.

EUNICE: Call Zoe. I'd like to have her down here, if she would like to come.

PENDAKIS: Alright, Eunie, I'll make the phone call.

*(*PENDAKIS *gets up and walks to the telephone. A* GUARD *walks in with an out of order sign in his hand.)*

GUARD: Eh, it ain't working.

(PENDAKIS *slams the receiver down.*)

PENDAKIS: *Malaka!*

(PENDAKIS *exits.* GUARD *runs after* PENDAKIS.)

GUARD: *Malaka?* What the hell does that mean?

(*During the above, a Japanese woman,* MRS SATO, *has entered the Emergency Room. She is a small woman dressed in a very shabby housedress, shabby to the point of rags. She wears a dirty kerchief about her head and carries in her hands two shopping bags. The shopping bags are crammed with the belongings of her life. On top of one of the bags is an old rag doll with the stuffing falling out of it. She is in her late fifties or early sixties, but, for all that matter, she may be a hundred years old. From her appearance, speech, and mannerisms, there is no doubt that the woman is half-crazed and is considered to be something of a daily nuisance by the hospital* NURSE *who barely acknowledges her presence.*)

MRS SATO: Have you seen my baby? Is my baby here?

GEORGE: *(To* NIKOS*)* Nicky, you want to take the elevator up? You think they'll stop us? We'll tear up the place.

MRS SATO: *(To* NIKOS*)* Please, mister, have you seen my baby?

TAKIS: Why isn't this Jap locked up with the rest of them?

NIKOS: *(Approaching* TAKIS*)* Look, lady, get lost. We've got our own problems to worry about. Just don't bother us.

MRS SATO: They took my baby up into the air and she melted all away.

(*The* NURSE *takes* MRS SATO's *arm.*)

NURSE: Come over here, Mrs. Sato. You sit over here today.

MRS SATO: *(Sits down)* I sat here all day yesterday and nobody came.

NURSE: *(To* MRS SATO*)* Of course, your granddaughter's all right. We told you that yesterday.

MRS SATO: *(Holds up the doll)* I brought this for her.

NIKOS: Looks like she found it in the garbage.

TAKIS: Bunch of slanty eyes.

*(*GEORGE *has crossed to the nurse's station, and picks up the* NURSE*'s chair and threatens to dash it against the desk.)*

GEORGE: Hey, lady, why don't you get us a doctor?

NURSE: *(Rushing off)* I'm getting him right now.

GEORGE: That's what I thought... That's the Greek way.

EUNICE: Will you shut up? All of you.

TAKIS: Calm down, Eunie.

EUNICE: You calm down.

TAKIS: Sarandaris is the one to get... That's what I say.

NIKOS: Yeah, which race is he running in?

MRS SATO: I sat here all day yesterday and nobody came for me at all....

ELAINE: Maybe you have the wrong bus stop.

*(*GEORGE *pulls* ELAINE *away.)*

GEORGE: Get away from this Jap.

*(*MRS SATO *clasps the rag doll to her breast.* PHILIP *enters.* PHILIP *is the twelve year old son of* EUNICE *and* NIKOS*. He is dressed in his ordinary school clothes.)*

TAKIS: *(Replying to* NIKOS*)* Whatever race Sarandaris is running in, I won't get a chance to bet it.

NIKOS: Maybe you'll save some money for a change.

PHILIP: Hi Mom! What's everybody doing here?

EUNICE: Philip!

NIKOS: What are you doing here?

EUNICE: *(Embraces her son)* Philip, are you alright?

ELAINE: What happened to you?

PHILIP: Let go will ya?

NIKOS: Shake his head and see if anything's rattling around.

PHILIP: I've got a couple of scratches. That's all.

HOSPITAL LOUD SPEAKER: Will Doctor Stevens report to the operating room?

ELAINE: Don't you know you nearly frightened us all to death?

GEORGE: Why is he holding his head like that?

(PHILIP takes his Uncle TAKIS' army hat and tries it on.)

NIKOS: Like what? What do you mean?

(PHILIP crosses toward MRS SATO.)

MRS SATO: You like Joltin' Joe?

PHILIP: *(Indicates MRS SATO)* Who's she?

NIKOS: Some Japanese lady. Now get your ass here so we can look at your head. Your uncle George thinks you're not holding it properly.

EUNICE: *(To PHILIP)* Philip, what did the doctor say?

TAKIS: *(To PHILIP)* I hope you're happy. You cost me the daily double.

PHILIP: What are they letting Japs in here for.

EUNICE: *(Embarrassed)* Philip!

MRS SATO: *(Holds out the doll)* I brought this for my granddaughter.

(PENDAKIS re-enters.)

NIKOS: Lady, get lost, will ya?

PENDAKIS: I called Zoe and she said she'd meet us down here... *(Sees* PHILIP*)* ...What in the hell is he doing up?

EUNICE: Philip, did the Doctor say it was alright for you to come down, or what?

PHILIP: You all didn't have to come down here. I take falls worse than that all the time.

PENDAKIS: Did you see Yannis when you were up there?

PHILIP: Gimme a quarter.

PENDAKIS: I'll give you kick in the ass.

GEORGE: Quarter, quarter, quarter. Where is he learning all that?

NIKOS: Let's take one thing at a time. Please!

(There is a brief silence.)

MRS SATO: Every day for a month I pray the president will save us, but now it is too late.

(Everyone stares at MRS SATO.*)*

MRS SATO: The American come with their big bombs and blow everything away.

GEORGE: I don't like the way he's walking.

MRS SATO: Not even a shadow is left.

*(*CAPTAIN HARRISON *stares at* MRS SATO *and then gets up and exits.)*

TAKIS: He's alright. Leave the kid alone.

PHILIP: Are you people coming with me or not? Or we going to spend the whole day here?

NIKOS: Let me at him... *(To* PHILIP*)* ...If your neck isn't broken now, it will be when I get through with it.

EUNICE: Nikos, stop it! You don't even know if he's alright or not.

NIKOS: (*Shouting at* PHILIP) What the hell is the matter with you? Scaring the life out of your mother and me like that.

ELAINE: For chrissakes, Nikos, he didn't do it on purpose.

NIKOS: Hell, he had no business up there on the roof in the first place.

EUNICE: I want to talk to the doctor myself.

NIKOS: I just want to get Philip home and beat the shit out of him, that's what I want to do.

GEORGE: Calm down, Nicky.

TAKIS: Giving us all a head-ache.

EUNICE: Sit down, Philip. I want to examine your head...Nikos!

NIKOS: Sit down when your momma tells you to.

PHILIP: Alright, but if Uncle Takis wants to see it, it's going to cost him a quarter.

GEORGE: (*To* TAKIS) You see what you're teaching the kid?

TAKIS: Me?

(*The* NURSE *has re-entered*).

NURSE: What's he doing here? He's supposed to be upstairs!

(NURSE *crosses to* MRS SATO, *who is kneeling on the floor.*)

NURSE: Get off the floor, Mrs Sato.

NIKOS: (*Confronting the* NURSE) You go get a doctor. You get a doctor down here and I mean it. Right now.

NURSE: (*Exiting*) Don't let him go. I'm calling Doctor Carrus.

GEORGE: We're finally going to get a damn doctor.

ELAINE: Philip, what did you do?

EUNICE: Nikos, didn't you hear what the nurse said? Philip isn't supposed to be down here.

PHILIP: It's O K, Ma. I'm alright, I tell you.

TAKIS: He looks O K to me.

NIKOS: *(To* TAKIS*)* What are you? A doctor all of a sudden?

NURSE: *(Voiceover)* Paging Doctor Carrus… Will Doctor Carrus please report to the Emergency Room at once?

ELAINE: *(To* PHILIP*)* Did you just walk out or what?

EUNICE: Philip?

NIKOS: For God's sake, don't shake him.

EUNICE: I'm not shaking him.

ELAINE: Philip, answer your mother.

(The NURSE *has returned.)*

NURSE: Your son can't leave the hospital.

(The men advance on the NURSE.*)*

PENDAKIS: Who says? He belongs to us, not to you.

NIKOS: You've got one of my sons as a hostage. Isn't one enough?

TAKIS: I wouldn't let Carrus work on a dead horse.

NIKOS: *(To* NURSE*)* And my brother-in-law should know. Those are the kind of horses he bets on.

PHILIP: I want to go home.

*(*PHILIP *has broken away from his mother's grasp and leaps over the prostrate form of* MRS SATO. GEORGE *catches* PHILIP *and holds him, blocking his escape.)*

EUNICE: Philip, you don't jump over somebody while they're praying. Can't you see she's praying? Apologize.

PHILIP: *(Mumbles)* I'm sorry.

EUNICE: Apologize!

PHILIP: *(Louder)* I'm sorry.

NIKOS: He's got the manners of an antelope.

NURSE: Please! He's got to sit down before he hurts himself.

NIKOS: He should have thought of that a couple of hours ago.

NURSE: He's got to wait for the doctor.

PENDAKIS: He needs a good spanking. That's what he needs.

NIKOS: *(To PENDAKIS)* Don't look at me. It's not my fault his mother doesn't give him any discipline.

EUNICE: That's right. I'm to blame for everything.

ELAINE: Will you two stop it?

GEORGE: Philip, sit down and act your age.

PHILIP: I'm sitting down... Alright?

NURSE: Doctor Carrus will be here in a minute.

NIKOS: Sure. Sure. Look for him in the bar.

PENDAKIS: I told Zoe to meet us here, so if you people are going home, I'm going to have to stay.

GEORGE: We came together. We'll leave together.

PHILIP: I want to go home.

NIKOS: *(To his son)* Skasmos!

PENDAKIS: There's not going to be enough room in one car anyway.

TAKIS: I told you we should have taken Angelo's car like I said.

PENDAKIS: Like you said. When Angelo sees how you're wrecked his car, he's going right through the ceiling

NIKOS: Forget it, I've already got a son that went right through the ceiling.

PHILIP: You should have seen the look on Johnny Vernalis' face. He thought I was dead.

ELAINE: I bet that thrilled him.

MRS SATO: (Loudly) You don't bury all the children in the earth. You bury them inside the flesh of their mothers. You cut open our skin. That's where you find our children.

NURSE: Mrs. Sato, stop it.

TAKIS: She ought to be in a loony bin.

NIKOS: I got some other people that ought to be in a loony bin too.

(MAX enters. it has been a struggle for him to reach the hospital, but he's made it.)

MAX: Well I made it. I finally found out where you boys was going.

(PHILIP runs to MRS SATO, and pretends to fire a machine gun at her.)

TAKIS: Philip!

PHILIP: Take that, you Jap.

EUNICE: Philip!

(PHILIP tosses his imaginary gun away and rushes out of the Emergency Room.)

PENDAKIS: Get him, Max!

(ELAINE, GEORGE, NIKOS, PENDAKIS, *and* TAKIS *run after* PHILIP *who has run from the hospital.*)

MAX: Wait a minute! I'm not running after you boys again!

(*We hear the sounds of the family chasing* PHILIP. *Lights are dimming. We hear the sounds of planes flying over the hospital. the sound brings* MRS SATO *to her feet. She looks at* CAPTAIN HARRISON *who has re-entered the waiting room.*)

MRS SATO: One hundred thousand dead. Isn't that enough for you people?

CAPTAIN HARRISON: Sorry, lady.

(CAPTAIN HARRISON *exits, allowing the waiting room doors to swing angrily behind him.*)

MRS SATO: Nobody hears the crying. Nobody hears… Nobody hears.

(MRS SATO *begins to gather up her bags. She exits. Lights are cross fading. End of scene*)

Scene 4

(*We are in* YANNIS' *hospital room.* NIKOS *is standing. He watches his son and wife sleep. He carries a small package in his hand.*)

EUNICE: Huh!

NIKOS: What?

EUNICE: Nicky…you scared me.

NIKOS: Me?

EUNICE: You.

NIKOS: Just watching you sleep. It's nice watching you two together. You're beginning to snore, you know.

EUNICE: Me?

NIKOS: You.

EUNICE: What about you?

NIKOS: Yea you.

EUNICE: Philip? ...What's happened to Philip?

NIKOS: He's alright...a little sprain in the neck, that's all. They're gonna put his neck in a brace, if they can get him to stand still long enough. Then they'll send him home and see how much more damage he can cause.

(EUNICE *notices the packages*)

NIKOS: ...Oh...a present from Max. He sent it over for Yannis.

EUNICE: What is it?

NIKOS: A book...some Kraut fairy tales or something. Yannis too old for them, but Max doesn't know these things.

EUNICE: Well, I hope you didn't tell him that.

NIKOS: I'll tell him you and Yannis danced for joy, alright... They got nice pictures in there...what's the matter...why doesn't he eat his food?

EUNICE: He can't.

NIKOS: *(By the hospital tray of food)* First, they got the red pills and the green pills, now the yellow pills. What the yellow pills for?

EUNICE: I don't know any more than you do, Nicky.

NIKOS: Never any white pills. White ones are the cheap ones. Take some aspirin, sprinkle a little color over it, and all of a sudden it's a miracle drug costing an arm and a leg....

(EUNICE *crosses to* NIKOS *to show him something in the book.*)

NIKOS: ...yeah, and look at the pictures here.

YANNIS: *(Mumbling in his sleep)* Arman
damonmyotamarmamrayarmtaramanrman...

NIKOS: He's saying something. What's he saying?

EUNICE: *(Quieting her son)* Shh...darling...shh... It's
soothing, it's just talk.

YANNIS: Iiiwan go ho ehme...

NIKOS: He's saying I want something. What do you
want, Yanni? *(To EUNICE)* Can't you hear him saying he
wants something?

EUNICE: *(Losing control)* It's just talk Nicky. He's been
running a fever all day.

NIKOS: Has he been able to keep anything in his
stomach?

EUNICE: A little.

NIKOS: A little. What's a little?

EUNICE: Nicky, you're giving me a headache.

NIKOS: Why don't you answer me when I ask you a
question?

EUNICE: I'm not used to having you ask, that's why...
Look Nicky, I don't know any more than you do.

NIKOS: You look tired Eunie. Why don't you take
Philip home, alright? I'll have Elaine come up here and
she can watch over Yanni.

EUNICE: I don't want anyone coming up. What do I
want more people coming up for? Yannis doesn't want
them. I don't want them.

NIKOS: I just asked that's all... Are you hungry?

EUNICE: No.

NIKOS: I can go out and get you something from the
cafeteria.

EUNICE: I'm not hungry... I've been nibbling off of Yannis' tray.

NIKOS: There must be something I can do. What can I do?

EUNICE: You want to do something? Take Philip to church this weekend. That's something for you to do.

NIKOS: What good does it do? The last time I took him, he spent his time counting the bricks on the wall.

EUNICE: Well do something with him. You're his father.

NIKOS: What's he going to do with his neck in a brace? What am I going to do?

EUNICE: Take him to the movies.

NIKOS: I'm sick of the goddamn movies.

EUNICE: Your son isn't.

NIKOS: There has to be more to life than movies and comic books.

EUNICE: He's frightened for Yannis.

NIKOS: He's frightened for Yannis. Good. Then tell him to get in line right behind me...frightened for Yannis.

EUNICE: You don't want to do anything with him do you?

NIKOS: I'll take him parachute jumping. Is that what you want?

EUNICE: *(Afraid that* YANNIS *will wake up)* Shhh!

NIKOS: No. I don't want to do anything with him... What the hell are you talking about?

EUNICE: Sometimes I think if it weren't for the boys, I would have left here a long time ago.

NIKOS: What are you saying? Where would you go? There's no place to go.

EUNICE: Maybe, I'd find someplace.

NIKOS: You whole family is here.

YANNIS: *(Begins squirming heavily)* Armanamarman-mamtarmantamrmanmamorarm...

EUNICE: I'm sorry Nicky...

NIKOS: Well...

(Lights down. End of scene.)

Scene 5

(There is a slow cross-fade from hospital room to the waiting room. The various members of the Janetakis family are still waiting. Reading Captain Marvel comic book, PHILIP sits scrunched in one corner. His neck is now in a brace. MAX sits off by himself and quietly studies the Old Testament that he always carries with him.)

GEORGE: *(Has an idea)* Hey, Foscolo! She has lots of chickens.

PENDAKIS: *(To TAKIS)* That's right. Got to Foscolo's.

TAKIS: Rita Foscolo? I went to school with her. I tried to take her out once, but her wop brothers beat the shit out of me. Remember that time we over-turned one of their cars out on Merrimac Street?

(NIKOS enters.)

PHILIP: Hi, Pop.

ELAINE: Nicky, is Eunie coming down?

NIKOS: Eunie? No. She's gone off to the train station to check the schedule.

PENDAKIS: Well? How's Yanni, Nikos?

MAX: Maybe I can get you some coffee or something?

NIKOS: *(To MAX)* What the hell are you hanging around here for?

PENDAKIS: You crazy? You got to pick on everybody?

NIKOS: I'm not picking on everybody. Just Max. Who the hell asked him to follow us down here? I didn't ask him to follow us down here.

ELAINE: Please, Nicky! Have some decency. He bought your son a present.

NIKOS: Present? Sure. A lousy dollar book. Some present. For a lousy dollar book, Pendakis is supposed to knock a thousand dollars off the restaurant.

PENDAKIS: There isn't going to be any restaurant if I don't get some chickens tonight.

MAX: You're asking three thousand dollars too much.

NIKOS: Who says? Ask anybody here if Pendakis is asking three thousand dollars too much?

MAX: What do you mean ask anybody here? You outnumber me five to one, six to one, if you count him. *(Pointing to* PHILIP.*)*

PHILIP: Thanks.

MAX: You're welcome.

NIKOS: So get somebody on your own side.

MAX: There is no one. Max Abrahamson is alone in this world, and he's not going to let a bunch of thieves walk all over me.

PENDAKIS: *Pau…pau…pau…* Max…

NIKOS: Oh yeah, Max… You gotta save that little speech there for John Foster Dulles…cause he's gonna bring everybody in the whole world together…yeah… Everybody is gonna gather somewhere in some great big ballroom and do a little dance… yeah…everybody is gonna be dancing and singing and clapping and not one person, not one person, not one person, Mister Max Abrahamson, is gonna give a shit that I have a ten year old kid upstairs who don't have a week left to live because of some goddamn...disease.

PENDAKIS: Nicky!...

PHILIP: Pa!

NURSE: Please! You must keep it quiet here. You're not the only people waiting here.

NIKOS: You... You...up your fongu with a wet noodle...

NURSE: *(Exiting)* I'm getting the Doctor, the police if I have to. *(She runs out.)*

NIKOS: Good. At last we're gonna get a doctor down here. It'll be the first time all day that a doctor has shown any interest in us. Not counting wrestling with my son in the parking lot.

ELAINE: We're gonna take Philip home with us.

NIKOS: Good. take him home.

PHILIP: No. I want to stay here.

NIKOS: No, you can't stay here. Go home.

ELAINE: Come on, get your stuff together.

GEORGE: Don't worry, Philip. Yannis is going to be alright.

NIKOS: Yeah, can't you see what time it is? You've got school in the morning.

PHILIP: You got work in the morning.

NIKOS: So I'm bigger than you. I don't need as much sleep.

GEORGE: *(To PHILIP)* I'm gonna drop you off at school in the morning myself.

NIKOS: Sell him on the open market for all I care. What's he been to me today but a pain in the ass... *(To PHILIP)* And if you don't stop snapping that gum of

yours, I'm going to wrap it around your neck and hang
you with it—brace and all.

PHILIP: I want to stay here.

*(NIKOS, in a brief burst of anger, starts to rearrange some
waiting room furniture.)*

NIKOS: You want to stay here? Sure, why not. Stay
here. It's almost like home. We'll have a pajama party.
It's almost like home anyway. I'm surprised they
haven't asked me to take a second mortgage out on this
place.

ELAINE: Nicky!

GEORGE: Nicky, how much longer is Eunie going to be
up there?

PENDAKIS: George!

NIKOS: I don't know…I don't know…I don't know…
Now stop asking me this for now. She may be up there
all night for all I know. What do I know?

ELAINE: Somebody's got to look after Philip too.

PHILIP: I can look after myself…SHAZAM…

ELAINE: Shazam yourself.

PENDAKIS: Nicky, take Philip home and both of you get
some sleep. If Takis gets the chickens, I can stay.

NIKOS: And what if Yannis needs another transfusion
tonight?

GEORGE: The hospital isn't going to run out of blood.

NIKOS: *Nikala!*

PHILIP: I can give blood, Pa!

PENDAKIS: I'll stay here. If Eunie needs anything, I'll get
it for her…

GEORGE: You're falling asleep on your feet…Nicky.

NIKOS: I'm not falling asleep.

GEORGE: Yes, you are.

NIKOS: I'm afraid to fall asleep... Don't you understand that?

PHILIP: I can't go to school tomorrow. I've got a broken neck. I can't even stand up...

TAKIS: Philip, quit horsing around.

GEORGE: We're all here, Nicky...

ELAINE: And we all do give a shit, Nicky.

(Pause.)

NIKOS: Look, why don't you all go home. There's nothing you can do here. *(To* PHILIP*)* Go with your Uncle George, Philip.

GEORGE: *(To* PHILIP*)* Yeah. You come home with me. *(To* ELAINE*)* Give me the keys.

NIKOS: After school, I'll drive by and pick you up, and we can come down here and see Yannis.

PHILIP: Promise?

NIKOS: Promise.

*(*ELAINE *pulls on her gloves.)*

GEORGE: *(To* ELAINE*)* What are you doing?

ELAINE: I'm going home with you and Philip.

GEORGE: Nothing for you to do there.

ELAINE: Where is there something for me to do?

GEORGE: *(Grabs* ELAINE's *arm)* Here...you're supposed to go upstairs and sit with Eunie. That's what you're supposed to do.

PENDAKIS: George.

GEORGE: Philip, come on.

PHILIP: SHAZAM...Solomon for Wisdom, Hercules for Strength, Atlas for stamina, Zeus for power,

(GEORGE *picks* PHILIP *up under one arm and carries* PHILIP *off.*)

PHILIP: Achilles for Courage, and Mercury for Speed…

GEORGE: Shazam your ass.

(GEORGE *and* PHILIP *have gone.*)

PENDAKIS: *(To* TAKIS*)* Hey you, stupid, go back to the restaurant and pick up the truck. I'll stay here with Nikos.

NIKOS: Nobody has to stay here with me.

TAKIS: How am I supposed to find Rita's place?

PENDAKIS: It's the only blue house out there.

TAKIS: How am I supposed to find a blue house at night?

MAX: Maybe you could listen for the chickens?

NIKOS: Cluck, cluck, Max.

PENDAKIS: We can't go more than seven centers a pound. Start with four.

MAX: At last, I'm learning something about the restaurant business.

NIKOS: Max, stay with us, and we'll get you to the top.

PENDAKIS: I want as many as I can get.

TAKIS: I can't drive a truck-load of chickens all by myself.

NIKOS: Take Max with you. He wants to learn the business.

PENDAKIS: *(To* NIKOS*)* You going to be alright?

NIKOS: Don't worry about me. I want to be alone.

PENDAKIS: You don't want to be alone. Who you trying to fool?

NIKOS: I'm trying to fool God, that's who.

PENDAKIS: Good luck! Max, you go with Charlie. I'll pay you.

MAX: I can't go.

PENDAKIS: Why not?

MAX: Because I don't know how to drive, that's why not.

PENDAKIS: It's alright, Max. You don't have to drive to be in the restaurant business.

NIKOS: You'll be so rich, you'll taxi everywhere.

TAKIS: Why don't we bring the chickens in by taxi?

NIKOS: Chickens have feet. They can march in by themselves.

PENDAKIS: Alright. I'll get George to drive. Zoe can look after Philip, and I can come back here.

NIKOS: I don't need a convention here.

PENDAKIS: A family isn't a convention.

(TAKIS *exits, followed by* PENDAKIS.)

NIKOS: This one is!

(*The* NURSE *enters, followed by a uniformed hospital* GUARD. *He is an elderly man of deep New England stock.*)

NURSE: (*Points toward* NIKOS) He's the one causing all the trouble!

NIKOS: I'm causing all the trouble! That's a good one. Tell it to my kid upstairs.

NURSE: He used vile language toward me...

(MAX *stands up and crosses toward the* GUARD.)

GUARD: (*To* NIKOS) Come here, mister!

MAX: It's not his fault, officer. It's my fault... All the yelling and the shouting.

(The GUARD *has removed his hat, and* MAX *uses that moment to slip a five dollar bill into it.)*

MAX: That was me. Nikos had nothing to do with it.

GUARD: Well, I'm giving you a warning.

NURSE: A warning!

GUARD: *(Staring out).* A fair warning, mister.

*(*NURSE *follows after the* GUARD.*)*

NURSE: You know what he said to me? He told me to fondle a noodle!

(The NURSE *has banged the top of the radio that is by her station and the radio comes on… She lowers the volume and exits. The dialogue continues between* MAX *and* NIKOS *while there is a cross-fade to* YANNIS' *hospital room on the upper level where* EUNICE *and* ELAINE *sit by* YANNIS' *bed. It is late at night.)*

ELAINE: Eunie?

EUNICE: *(Barely awake)* What?

ELAINE: You go home.

EUNICE: No. I'm alright.

ELAINE: I'll stay and watch Yannis.

EUNICE: *(Adjusting* YANNIS' *bed-covering.)* I'm not tired.

ELAINE: Should I get Nicky?

EUNICE: Nicky?

ELAINE: He's still downstairs?

EUNICE: Is he? I thought everybody had gone home.

ELAINE: Why would you think that?

EUNICE: But what about Philip? Where's Philip? Who's looking after Philip?

ELAINE: Eunie, Eunie, keep calm…Philip is fine. He went home with George.

EUNICE: With George?

ELAINE: Or somewhere with George. George is looking after him.

NIKOS: Max, turn off the radio, huh?

EUNICE: Philip is getting shuttled around a lot lately.

ELAINE: Who isn't?...

(EUNICE *looks offended.*)

ELAINE: I didn't mean it like that, Eunie. for Chrissakes, we love having Philip. You know that.

EUNICE: Outside of Captain Marvel, he hasn't read a book all summer.

ELAINE: You want George to make him read? George'll make him read.

EUNICE: Nicky should make him read...maybe if Nicky talked to him.

ELAINE: To George?

EUNICE: To Philip. He can't run around wild all summer.

ELAINE: Nobody listens to me. Maybe he'll listen to George.

(MRS SATO *can be seen in the doorways to* YANNIS' *hospital room. She is carrying a pathetic rag doll.*)

ELAINE: *(Alerting* EUNICE*)* Eunie.

(EUNICE *stands and protects her child upon seeing* MRS SATO.*)

MRS SATO: It's alright...alright...no harm...no harm... (*She puts the metal guard to* YANNIS' *bed up.*)

ELAINE: What are you doing?

MRS SATO: I'm gonna put this up...and stay on this side...everything hunky dory. I'm Mrs. Sato. I met you downstairs.

EUNICE: Yes, I remember.

MRS SATO: I'm looking for my granddaughter…I brought this for her… *(Waving the filthy doll)*

EUNICE: It's very nice.

ELAINE: But she isn't here lady.

MRS SATO: Oh no, she isn't here. I can see that…

(YANNIS stirs.)

MRS SATO: …Only boy on this floor.

EUNICE: Yes, only boys.

ELAINE: *(To* EUNICE*)* Should I get the nurse?

EUNICE: No.

MRS SATO: Yes, sleeping… Your son sleeps so good. It is a blessing to sleep so good.

EUNICE: Yes.

MRS SATO: Good looking boy like the one downstairs?

EUNICE: *(To* ELAINE*)* Downstairs? Is Philip still downstairs?

MRS SATO: Oh no. They've all gone home.

EUNICE: Oh.

ELAINE: You betcha.

EUNICE: Sure, she has boys.

MRS SATO: I waited all day yesterday and nobody came.

ELAINE: We heard that one before lady.

MRS SATO: They say she isn't here, but I know she is.

EUNICE: Maybe on another floor. *(She sees* MRS SATO *look at the tray of uneaten food.)* …Take the food if you want.

ELAINE: No, Eunie.

EUNICE: Yanni can't eat it.

ELAINE: Oh boy. Nicky is going to kill us.

MRS SATO: I don't make trouble for anyone...

(MRS SATO *takes the food and then begins to recite a prayer for* YANNIS...*the ladies listen and look intently.*)

MRS SATO:
Chin Chin Kobokama
Yomo fuke soro
Oshizumare, Himi Gimi
Ya ton ton.

(YANNIS *stirs slightly.* EUNICE *and* ELAINE *lean over to see if anything has happened,* EUNICE *turns quickly and is frightened by* ELAINE *who is staring over* EUNICE'S *shoulder.*)

EUNICE: Oh Elaine.

ELAINE: *(Threatening)* For Christ sakes lady, get out of here before I call the police.

MRS SATO: *(Leaving the food on a stool)* I go...I don't make trouble for anyone. *(She exits.)*

EUNICE: *(Calls after her)* Mrs Sato!! Elaine, what did you do that for?

ELAINE: Me! Why do you let anybody off the street come in and take anything they want?

EUNICE: She only wanted the food. Yannis can't eat it.

ELAINE: You're paying for it... And what was that mumbo-jumbo stuff anyway?

EUNICE: Some poetry I guess. *(Tucking in* YANNIS' *blanket)*

ELAINE: Poetry? That's what you thought it was... *(Proudly)* Mister Moon can make you swoon.

(ELAINE *and* EUNICE *laugh as they both say the last line together.*)

ELAINE & EUNICE: But Miss Vaughn will make you yawn…

ELAINE: That' s my kind of poetry. You know that, Eunie?

EUNICE: Of course: You had Mrs Vaughn?

ELAINE: Not me. I had Mrs Cam for English, and Mister Barrows… You know it's funny, half the time you can't even remember your neighbors' names.

EUNICE: Mrs Vaughn… God help us… When she got onto poetry she was something.

ELAINE: I had a crush on Mister Barrows. I let him look up my dress a little, and he let me pass English a little.

(EUNICE *is startled*.)

ELAINE: It's just a joke, Eunie… It was a long time ago… Don't you tell anyone, Eunie.

EUNICE: Don't worry, I won't… Do you remember *Thanatopsis*?

ELAINE: Who's he?

EUNICE: It's a poem, Elaine by William Cullen Bryant.

ELAINE: Oh.

EUNICE: I was the first one in Mrs Vaughn's class to get it memorized.

ELAINE: Of course.

EUNICE: …And I remember how excited I was. I couldn't wait to get to school the next day to tell her. I knew she thought that *Thanatopsis* was the most beautiful poem ever written…I don't know how I got out of the house so early, but I must have arrived at Wamesit High School about six-thirty in the morning and waited for her in the parking lot, and when I saw her drive up, I ran to her… I didn't let her get out of the car or anything..."Mrs Vaughn, I've got it memorized! I've got it memorized!...

ELAINE: *(Quieting* EUNICE*)* Shhh...don't worry Eunie, he likes it...

EUNICE: ...I can even tell you what she was wearing that day...

ELAINE: *(Proudly)* What Eunie?

EUNICE: She had on a long dark purple dress and a hat with a veil rolled back onto the brim... And I didn't let her get out of the car or anything... "To him who in the love of Nature holds/Communion with her visible forms, she speaks a various language..." On and on through the whole eighty-one lines, and all the while there were people passing us...but she didn't even move. She sat there, listening, and then she got out of the car, and she hugged me...Elaine... In front of everyone Elaine, she hugged me...Elaine...

NIKOS: *(Lying on a bench)* Alright Max. You win.

EUNICE: Hug me now.

(The women embrace gently.)

NIKOS: You can read to me if you want...

ELAINE: Eunie, how do you memorize all that poetry.. you must be smart...huh...

(The lights cross-fade from YANNIS*'s room to the waiting room.)*

MAX: No you're not interested.

NIKOS: Of course I'm interested. A few more days around here and I'd be interested in stamp collecting.. Come on, Max. Find a dirty part. The Bible is full of dirty parts, and don't tell me it isn't because I know... With all those begets and begets... Just talk to me so that I know somebody else is still here.

MAX: You want me maybe to talk about the restaurant business?

NIKOS: At one o'clock in the morning? No, I don't want to talk about the restaurant business. Besides, it's my brother-in-law's business, not mine! ...I want religion. I want true-blue religion, I want to see the hand of God at the end of the rainbow...clutching a hundred dollar win ticket on Dead to Rights.

(MAX *doesn't respond.* GUARD *enters.*)

NIKOS: Alright, then. Come on, we'll talk about Jake La Motta... You want to talk about Jake La Motta. You know how much money that bum cost me? Nobody in their right mind bets on the fighters, Max. Always bet on the horses. At least you know they're human... *(He yawns.)* ...Christ!

MAX: Nikos, you go home and get some rest...I'll wait here.

NIKOS: What are the hell you talking about? You'll wait here. Who in the hell are you to wait here?

MAX: I'm Max...I'm your friend Max...I'm here because I'm here.

NIKOS: Yeah, well I'm Nikos...and I'm here because I'm here.. And I'm gonna stay here...and we're not gonna talk about this no more.

(MAX *opens his old testament and begins to read. First in Hebrew and then translating for* NIKOS.)

NIKOS: *(While* MAX *is reading in Hebrew)* That's right Maxey...sing a little song...

MAX: *(After finishing the Hebrew)* ...They came to the place which had been told to them by God...and there Abraham built an altar and laid the wood...and took Isaac his son...and laid him on the altar above the wood...and Abraham stretched forth his hand..and took the knife to slay his son...

NIKOS: Wait a minute...wait a minute... Hold it... What in the hell are you doing?

MAX: I'm reading to you like you said.

NIKOS: What do you mean like I said. What the hell do you listen to me for? Nobody else does. I don't want to hear that story. Read me another story. I know how it comes out.

MAX: *(Surprised)* You know it?

NIKOS: You don't think I know it? You think I'm illiterate or something. I know it...I'll tell you something else...that story is a bunch of crap... What the hell sense is there in some guy going around and killing off his own kid? It don't make no sense. If the parents go first, that's alright...that's the way things are supposed to be in this world...but the rest of that is a bunch of...the rest of that, Max, is just like the Ballroom in Saint Patrick's Cathedral... Hey Max, I bet you Jews don't know they got a ballroom in Saint Patrick's Cathedral.

MAX: No, I didn't know that.

NIKOS: You don't know it... You've seen pictures of it, haven't you?

MAX: I've seen pictures of the outside of it.

NIKOS: That's why it's so big. They got this great big ballroom inside of it. That's why there are so many Catholics, Max. They like to go dancing all the time.

MAX: I didn't know that either.

NIKOS: Hey Max, did I ever tell you about the time I went dancing in the ballroom in Saint Patrick's Cathedral?

MAX: No, you didn't.

NIKOS: It was about '32, '33, and I was living in New York then...forty-eight Greeks all sharing the same room... One Greek got a room, everybody got a room. We had people sleeping in the bathtub, on the floor, in the fire escape...one day the landlord stops me and my brothers on the stairs coming home from work and he says to me "How many you got in that room up there...how many you got?" "We got three. That's all just three." He looks at me and says... "Just three?" Goddamn place smells like a Turkish bath... you open the door, your sinuses clear up like that... So anyway we got me and my brothers, and about forty other Greeks floating in and out of this place, and we got one good suit between us, and one good pair of shoes... George Vrettakos... George Vretakkos... A big moose of a guy, you know, but he had little feets, so he and I wore the same size shoes. A beautiful pair of white bucks...Max...he must have stolen them from someplace... He was always walking in and out of coatrooms and closets. Light Fingers George we used to call him... Hey, George, bring your fingers over here... What the hell did it matter? It was the Depression, who cares? Anyway I got this date with this most beautiful woman from over at Birdland... I mean she was gorgeous. She had a rear end on her like could sink a battleship, so naturally I wanted to take her someplace special...some place she's never been before...really show her the good time...

MAX: The ballroom in Saint Patrick's Cathedral.

NIKOS: That's right, Max...the ballroom...and so while Moose is sleeping...I get dressed and sneak into George's room...stepping over a few Greeks...and takes the shoes, and I'm off...dancing up a storm... You should have seen me, Max... In my time, I was a dancer. Kids today, what the hell do they know about dancing... Do you know how to dance, Max?

MAX: Me? Dancing, schamcing.

NIKOS: I didn't think so...so there I am nestled to this girl's...what do you call them: *(He gestures.)*

MAX: Bazooms...

(CAPTAIN HARRISON, sitting at the back of the waiting room, begins to follow the dialogue between MAX and NIKOS.)

NIKOS: Yeah, well anyway the orchestra's playing, the lights are swirling... This place, Max... You've never seen...hundreds and hundreds of lights...everyone a different color...it's beautiful...and hundreds of people dancing on the ballroom, but we're not dancing on the floor, Max, we are dancing in the air...

(NIKOS begins whirling MAX around in a dance.)

NIKOS: ...around and around the ballroom floor, we're dancing.

(MAX sees the GUARD coming down to see what all the noise is and he taps NIKOS on the shoulder to stop.)

NIKOS: ...Max, anyway, all of a sudden, you know, I feel this tap on the back of my shoulder, so naturally I think some wise ass wants to cut in, but when I turn around, there's my friend George. He is fit to be tied...I mean he's like a moose-ox...you know...He can tear me limb from limb... "Take off those shoes," he says. "You take off those shoes... Those are my shoes... My turn to wear the shoes and I have a date...

GUARD: *(Coming downstage.)* Alright. Alright here. This is a hospital here.

NIKOS: There's no reason to raise your voice.

(The GUARD leaves.)

MAX: So what did you do?

NIKOS: George took his shoes back, and left me
standing there in the middle of the ballroom floor
in my stocking feet…I tell you Max…I felt like the
smallest person in the whole wide world… My date,
my date by now…I'm trying to tell my date that this
guy is crazy, that he broke in and stole my shoes, but
I'm dead… She's looking at me like I'm dead. Those
battleships are going down, and I'm not on them…
she's looking at me like I'm dead… Did you ever try
walking across Manhattan in your stocking feet? It
could have been worse I suppose. He could have taken
his pants back… So anyway, that's what it's like.

MAX: What's like?

NIKOS: That's what it's like to go dancing in the
ballroom at Saint Patrick's Cathedral.

(MAX *cracks a sun-flower seed with his teeth.*)

MAX: Well, you shouldn't have taken your friend's
shoes.

(*Music swells. Lights out.*)

END OF ACT ONE

ACT TWO

Scene 1

(Several hours later. We see EUNICE *and* ELAINE *sitting on one bench, with* MRS SATO *occupying the floor in front of the other bench upon which* NIKOS *is sleeping on downstage.* MAX *is reading his Bible by the nurse's station.)*

CAPTAIN HARRISON: Excuse me, ladies…I'm going out for some coffee. Can I get you some?

EUNICE: Yes…thank you…

*(*CAPTAIN HARRISON *begins to leave.)*

EUNICE: …Black… *(To* MRS SATO*)* That's what I have to admit to myself. If I could die in his place, I could accept that, or if Nicky died. I wake up wishing that my husband should die and not my son, and if that' enough to send me to hell, then so be it, but don't you come in here with your crazy ideas what will harm us and what won't.

MRS SATO: I have daughter too… You help me find my daughter.

EUNICE: I'm sorry.

MRS SATO: I go look for my daughter upstairs…I am right to go on looking?

EUNICE: Oh, yes.

MRS SATO: It will work out for the best. Everything work out for the best.

EUNICE: That's what they say isn't it?

MRS SATO:
When I went out into the spring meadows
to gather violets,
I enjoyed myself so much,
that I stayed all night.
(She exits.)

EUNICE: She has her poetry and we have ours.

(They sit.)

NURSE: *(Crossing downstage).* Mrs Panayotopoulos, Doctor Carrus want to see you in his office about the test results.

EUNICE: *(To* ELAINE*)* I'll be right back... *(She tries to wake up* NIKOS.*)* Nicky...wakeup...Doctor Carrus wants to see us...

*(*CAPTAIN HARRISON *returns with the coffee.)*

EUNICE: ...Sorry, I have to go now...

MAX: *(Coming over to try and wake up* NIKOS*)* Wake up, Nikos.

Scene 2

(During MRS SATO*'s gift of poetry, lights have gradually been cross-fading to reveal the kitchen of* RITA FOSCOLO*'s farmhouse. We hear* TAKIS *yelling to his brother,* GEORGE.*)*

TAKIS: Hey, George, when you get out of that chicken coop, wipe your feet off.

GEORGE: *(off)* Okay, okay.

*(*TAKIS *and* RITA *enter,* GEORGE *soon follows.* TAKIS *and* GEORGE *seat themselves around a small kitchen table.* RITA *is a large black-haired Italian woman who is dressed in a simple house-robe that is so loosely tired that every once*

in a while, the top opens wide enough to reveal an ample
bosom. TAKIS *is in his uniform, and* GEORGE *is in his same*
costume as ACT ONE. Both, however, have unbuttoned
their shirts and have made themselves quite at home. Our
initial impression should be that the brothers have been
at the farmhouse for several hours and that drinking and
dancing have taken place. At least, an inexpensive Chianti is
being passed back and forth among them. From outside, we
can hear the sound of crickets.)

TAKIS: *(To* RITA*)* I got this joke. This guy has this pair of
shorts...undershorts...and they don't fit or anything...
okay...okay?

RITA: Okay.

TAKIS: *(To* GEORGE*)* What?

GEORGE: He goes into May's Department Store.

(It is obvious that TAKIS *is heavily intoxicated.)*

TAKIS: Right? ...Okay. So, he goes back. *(He forgets*
again.) Oh yeah..."I'm going to exchange these shorts."
So he goes back to the guy who sold him the shorts...

GEORGE: Ah...it was a girl...

TAKIS: Oh yea...it was a girl this time... So he says he
wants to exchange these shorts...I want to exchange
these shorts...so she looks at him like he's crazy or
something and she goes..."Why do you want to
exchange these shorts...why do you want to exchange
these shorts?"...so he says... Cause there's no Ballroom
in Saint Patrick's Cathedral... Don't you get it?

*(*RITA *is laughing at* TAKIS.*)*

TAKIS: ...There's no Ballroom in Saint Cathedral...
Come on, Rita...let's dance. *(She moves out of the rocker*
she was sitting on.) How 'bout a little kiss?

RITA: If I kiss you what will my husband think?

TAKIS: Your husband? You get married again?

RITA: You crazy. *(She laughs.)* Both of you crazy. I should never have let the two of you in her tonight... Takis, my husband has been dead for two years.

TAKIS: Oh, well...then I don't think he'd mind... You keep it locked up down there for two years, Rita, Rita..

RITA: *(To* GEORGE*)* You see how he talks to me. Your brother. He's got a screw loose somewhere to talk to me like that...

GEORGE: Hell, I have nothing to do with him.

RITA: If you really loved me, nothing would have kept you from it... Now I remember the one you got me confused with... It was that Papatsonis girl you were feeling up all the time...

TAKIS: Papatsonis?

RITA: The one that looked like an ironing board.

TAKIS: You think any girl who doesn't have bosoms that don't reach out to next year is like an ironing board... All you wops...you got this Alps fixation.

RITA: And I remember how you and her brother used to cheat like crazy on all the Latin examinations.

TAKIS: *(Crossing to the table for some more wine)* ...So what? I'm supposed to care about Latin? It's a dead language for Chris sakes. They could of taught me Greek...I could have made an A in Greek.

GEORGE: You couldn't make an A in nothing...Takis, I gotta go home...Elaine's going to go through the ceiling as is.

TAKIS: Wait a minute...I want to prove a point, Rita. You got a high school yearbook?

RITA: Yeah, I got a yearbook, but it's in the bedroom.

TAKIS: So what?

RITA: So we're not going into the bedroom.

TAKIS: Rita, we're not in high school anymore.

RITA: Takis, you want my chickens…you don't want me.

TAKIS: *(Pinching her as she passes to get some coffee.)* Oh, boy, will you listen to that?

RITA: Oh, a little sweet talk, a little feel, and you think I'm going to give you my chickens… Oh Takis…

TAKIS: Rita, listen, I only have a couple of days left on my leave…then they're going to ship me back someplace. I oughta get a little special consideration or something, don't you think?

GEORGE: Eisenhower should hear this…or Patton…

TAKIS: What's the harm in it? Just a little kiss… Come on…

RITA: *(Being chased around her table)* No!

TAKIS: One kiss, huh?…how 'bout a hug then?

RITA: *(Picking up her meat cleaver)* You take one more step and I cut everything off.

GEORGE: *(To RITA)* It's just gonna be a little cut.

TAKIS: *(Sitting on rocker)* Boy, Rita, I just thought for old times' sake.

GEORGE: You ain't old enough for old times.

RITA: *(At counter)* Old times? What old times? You and I never had any old times. I think you've got me confused with somebody else…

TAKIS: I don't have you mixed up with anybody else. I almost took you to the movies.

RITA: Takis, I'm supposed to get excited over that? Is that supposed to be the highlight of my life these last ten years?

GEORGE: It can't be the highlight of her life. She's got five kids in there, Takis.

TAKIS: *(To* RITA*)* It was your own family that kept us apart... Your beefy brothers with heads like ox... Blame them, not me! *(Fixing his tie)* George, look at this... Rita, when we first drove up here tonight, what was the first thing you said to me?

GEORGE: She...said, "Who's out there? What do you want?"...Damn it, Takis, I've got to go home.

TAKIS: You wait for me, George. I wait for you all the time.

GEORGE: You're not married.

TAKIS: It's not my fault. After you saw who it was... didn't you say I hadn't changed a bit?

RITA: You were standing in the dark. Nothing changes when you can't see it.

GEORGE: I'm going to sit in the truck.

TAKIS: So what do you want me to do about it?

GEORGE: So I want you to know that I'm not going to wait out there all night.

TAKIS: *(Pushing* GEORGE *out)* Rita, George is leaving now. He has an engagement... He's left.

GEORGE: *(After exiting)* Old times...

RITA: Takis, you think I'm so stupid I'm supposed to believe everything you and your brother tell me?

TAKIS: Yeah, well, Rita...you think I came out here because of Pendakis, right, for chickens? I didn't come out here for that...I came here because of me.

RITA: You think that I still look the same?

TAKIS: Yeah, sure you do...what are you going to do? You gonna let them blow the world out from underneath us, or what?

RITA: Suppose I get pregnant?

(TAKIS *checks the pocket of his shirt.*)

TAKIS: Ah, you wouldn't get pregnant.

RITA: I don't believe in taking precautions.

TAKIS: That only applies if you're married.

RITA: Who says?

RITA: The Pope (*She makes the sign of the cross.*) Never said any such thing.

TAKIS: You mean it's alright to fornicate and not alright for me to take precautions.

RITA: It's not alright. It's a sin. I'll have to confess. (*She crosses to the rocking chair.*)

TAKIS: What are you going to do? Let the Pope run your life? The world is filled with unwanted kids.

RITA: My children are not unwanted!

TAKIS: I didn't say your kids are unwanted, Rita.

RITA: Why don't you just get out of here. First, you insult me, and then you insult the Pope.

TAKIS: I wasn't insulting the Pope. I was just questioning things. I'm smart. I do that all the time. I have a mind that questions things.

RITA: What are you going to insult next? Huh? My chickens? ...Oh no because these are the best chickens in all New England...

TAKIS: We'll talk about the chickens in the morning. What do you think about that?

RITA: Oh no, we'll talk about them never. I'll sell them to the government, every pound of them... Now you get away from me...I wouldn't sell you my chickens if you were the last man on earth.

(Voices of two of RITA's *young children can be heard for off-stage.)*

RITA's CHILDREN: *(Suddenly awakened; offstage)* Mama... Mama...Mama...

RITA: Now you see what you made me do? You made me wake up my children...

TAKIS: Alright. Let life pass you by. See if I care...

RITA: You care, you care... Go look up the Papatsonis girl and see if she'll put out for you!...

TAKIS: Fine...Forget it...You want to sell your lousy chickens or not? I'll give you seven cents a pound...I mean four cents a pound...shit...

RITA: *(Holding out her breasts)* You wouldn't know what to do with these anyway...

*(*TAKIS *accidently knocks over the rocking chair. He gets hold of it and violently throws it down again.* TAKIS *exits.* RITA *picks the rocker up while we hear* GEORGE's *voice outside.)*

GEORGE: You go load those chickens in the truck. You gotta have chickens for a chicken restaurant. *(He enters.)* Rita...don't be mad... *(He holds out bottle of wine.)* Let's talk about chickens...

RITA: *(To* GEORGE) Go home...go home...

*(*GEORGE *blows her a kiss and then leaves.)*

RITA: Just don't talk about loving me...

(Night sounds. Lights fade to black. End of scene)

Scene 3

(The waiting room of the hospital. It is about an hour and a half later than the previous scene. In the waiting room are EUNICE, ELAINE, NIKOS, MAX, *and* MRS SATO. CAPTAIN HARRISON *and the* NURSE *are intently listening to the radio.)*

RADIO BROADCAST: ...Here is a bulletin... The White House has just announced that the Japanese Government has accepted the peace proposals of the Allied government... Stand by for further details. *(There is a pause, and then we hear a voice in Japanese, accompanied by an American translation.)* The Emperor will be required to insure that the Government of Japan and the Japanese Imperial Headquarters agree to the surrender terms necessary to carry out the provisions of the Potsdam declaration... This is the United State of America.

(Victory music... During the broadcast, CAPTAIN HARRISON *joyfully exits.)*

NIKOS: Shut off the radio, will you?

(The NURSE *shuts off the radio and exits.)*

NIKOS: I want to move Yannis to Boston.

EUNICE: What? Are you talking to us?

NIKOS: I said I want to move Yannis to Boston. All the experts are in Boston.

EUNICE: The last time we were in Boston, they wanted to amputate Yannis' leg.

NIKOS: We're not going to argue about it, alright? As soon as Yannis is well enough, we'll take him back to Boston. I'll find you an apartment down there and drive down to see you on weekends.

EUNICE: It's not so easy.

NIKOS: You think this is any easier?

EUNICE: And what about Philip? What are we going to do with Philip? Sweep him under the rug?

ELAINE: George and I can take Philip. And we can help you find an apartment.

EUNICE: We'll see. Yannis has missed too much school all ready.

NIKOS: Not we'll see! We're going to make a decision right now.

(MRS SATO *has brought out her belongings into the center of the waiting room floor. She begins to lay out about a dozen pair of baby shoes that she has collected from various sources.)*

EUNICE: Not now. I can't think now.

NIKOS: Yes, now. I'm sick and tired of the goddamn doctors telling us when we should bring him in, and when we should take him out. When he should take a piss.

ELAINE: Nicky, come on, face it. You have to do what the doctors say, you have no choice.

NIKOS: Don't tell me I got no choice. George's got no choice, you got no choice, but I got plenty of choice. So you just butt out.

(ELAINE *is stung by* NIKOS's *remark. She gets up and walks away.)*

ELAINE: I'm sorry.

NIKOS: *(Erupting)* You're sorry. Max is sorry. Everybody's sorry.

ELAINE: I'll wait outside.

EUNICE: Don't listen to him. You know how he gets.

NIKOS: That's right. Don't listen to me. Nobody listens to me.

ELAINE: I'll bring back some coffee.

NIKOS: Good. Get some coffee. Make yourself useful.

(ELAINE exits.)

EUNICE: There's no need to fight with Elaine.

(PENDAKIS enters.)

PENDAKIS: Well it's all over.

(From offstage in the hospital corridor, we can hear the voices of GEORGE and TAKIS.)

NIKOS: What's all over?

PENDAKIS: The war.

(CAPTAIN HARRISON has returned to the waiting room.)

NIKOS: That was over a long time ago.

GEORGE: *(Voice offstage)* Did you leave the windows open a crack?

(GEORGE and TAKIS, exuberant with the news of the war ending, enter. They shake hands, hug, kiss. There is general rough-housing.)

EUNICE: Takis?

TAKIS: What?

(EUNICE warmly embraces TAKIS. PENDAKIS joins them.)

TAKIS: *(To PENDAKIS)* You need a dishwasher?

GEORGE: Hell no. Pendakis is going to let you run the whole damn cash register.

(ELAINE re-enters with two cups of coffee. She crosses to GEORGE, and tries to tone-down the rough-housing.)

ELAINE: George...George... They're operating now.

TAKIS: We came as soon as we heard.

EUNICE: It's alright.

(GEORGE *crossing upstage to shake hands with* CAPTAIN HARRISON.)

GEORGE: Hey Nicky, I didn't even go back to the restaurant. I got a damn truckload of chickens out there. Zoe's watching the kids. (*To* PENDAKIS) Did Sarandaris get the message?

PENDAKIS: How do I know? I left messages all over the place. If he goes to the bathroom, he'll find it scribbled on the wall.

TAKIS: (*Noticing* MAX) Max, you still here?

NIKOS: What'd you think he was, a mirage?

MAX: Just keeping him company.

ELAINE: That should qualify you for sainthood, Max.

NIKOS: Sure. A Jewish Saint. Why not? We've got everything else down here.

(*Pause*)

GEORGE: Nicky, I'm sorry. I didn't...

TAKIS: What are they operating for? They said it was allergies.

EUNICE: No one knows.

NIKOS: She doesn't know what to do. I don't know what to do, you know?

PENDAKIS: We've got to wait it out, that's all. (*Motions to* TAKIS *to sit down*) Takis!

ELAINE: (*To* GEORGE) He went in over an hour ago. Yannis went into convulsions. They had to operate. Yannis was screaming down the hall, and where were you? I didn't know where you were.

GEORGE: I was doing business.

PENDAKIS: God help us.

TAKIS: Nicky, look, I can get Sarandaris for you on the phone if you just loan me a nickel. Alright?

NIKOS: What the hell's the matter with you? Your arm's too short to reach your pocket?

TAKIS: I just don't have a nickel, that's all.

(MAX *hands him a nickel.*)

ELAINE: *(To* GEORGE*)* Well? Did you have a good time at the chicken farm?

GEORGE: God damn it, I didn't touch the woman.

ELAINE: Why do you have that smell all over you?

GEORGE: You can't tell chicken shit from perfume?

PENDAKIS: George! Sit down.

TAKIS: *(To* ELAINE*)* I'll prove to you we were doing business out there. *(To* PENDAKIS*)* Here's your money back.

PENDAKIS: How much did you pay her?

TAKIS: Pay her? *(He crosses to* EUNICE*)* ...She doesn't even know they're missing.

PENDAKIS: Did you take the truck out to Foscolo's or not?

TAKIS: Well, we didn't go to Havana with it... *(He laughs.)*

GEORGE: Pendakis, let me tell you something about your little baby brother... Do you know what he was doing? Takis was inside that house charming the pants off Rita and I was out in the dirty chicken coop loading the dirty chickens onto the dirty truck.

TAKIS: Right!

PENDAKIS: You stole the chickens?

NIKOS: You stole the chickens?

PENDAKIS: You can't walk off with her chickens like that.

TAKIS: Why not? How is she going to prove they're hers?

PENDAKIS: Because they're like children to her. She probably has got them all marked.

TAKIS: How do you brand a chicken?

MAX: I can't serve my customers stolen chickens, Pendakis.

PENDAKIS: They're my customers, Max. You haven't bought the restaurant yet.

MAX: I'm trying, Mister Janetakis.

PENDAKIS: Good, Mister Abrahamson. *(To* TAKIS*)* Why didn't you pay her seven cents a pound like I told you?

TAKIS: Because she wouldn't sell them to us, that's why. What are you going to do? You're going to close down the restaurant because you're honest? Right?

NIKOS: Look who's talking about honesty?

PENDAKIS: How many chickens?

TAKIS: Our family has been honest our whole lives, and where has it gotten us?

PENDAKIS: How many chickens?

TAKIS: So what's the big deal over a few lousy chickens?

PENDAKIS: *(Shouting)* How many chickens?

GEORGE & TAKIS: One-hundred and twenty-eight!

PENDAKIS: You stole one-hundred and twenty-eight chickens?

GEORGE: We had better get a start plucking them so she can't identify them.

MRS SATO: *(To her rag doll)* Omae wa washi wo wasureta ta?

NIKOS: Pendakis, get her the hell out of here.

EUNICE: Leave her alone.

(MRS SATO picks up her baby shoes.)

NIKOS: She's getting on my nerves.

EUNICE: You're getting on everyone's nerves. You don't own this place.

MAX: Mrs Panayotopoulos, perhaps, I can get you a cup of coffee? Soda? Or something?

ELAINE: For God sakes, Max. Call her Eunie like everybody else, you don't have to be so formal all the time.

MAX: I'm sorry. Habit I guess.

NIKOS: Do any of you have any idea what it's like to wake up every morning with the same goddamn thought running through your head day after day after day? You think I've thought about anything else for the past six months? The goddamn doctors upstairs keep telling Eunie and me to expect the worst. Is there any way any of you can do that for me? ...The goddamn doctors up there want me to think that there's no hope.

EUNICE: Nicky, please.

NIKOS: Well, I got hope. I don't care what none of you say, I've got hope.

GEORGE: Nicky, did anyone say not to have hope? Did anyone say not to have hope?

PENDAKIS: If anybody did, I'd kick them in the teeth.

MRS SATO: *(To MAX)* I'm going to the cemetery now. You come with me?

NIKOS: I thought I told you to get her the hell out of here.

MAX *(To* MRS SATO*)* No, I'm just a friend of the family.

*(*NIKOS *lunges at* MRS SATO*.)*

NIKOS: I'll throw her out of here!

ELAINE: Nicky, what are you doing? You're not helping Yannis acting like that!

NIKOS: You know how to help him?

ELAINE: No…I don't.

*(*GEORGE *grabs* NIKOS *by the arms.)*

GEORGE: Nicky, Nicky…Calm down…calm down.

NIKOS: I'm alright.

MRS SATO: *(To* EUNICE*)* I didn't do anything.

EUNICE: It's alright…I know.

(The NURSE *enters. Her hair is dotted with chicken feathers.)*

NURSE: Are you the people with the chickens?

GEORGE; Don't answer that. You don't have to answer that. Who wants to know?

(The NURSE *wipes the bottom of her shoes.)*

NURSE: Look, I don't care whose chickens they are. I was just trying to help you people, that's all. I'm only a nurse here. I'm not trying to win the sainthood award.

(We become aware of some vast celebration going on offstage. A beginning V-J Day celebration, with fire-crackers going off, and shouting. Every once in awhile, we can hear the sound of chickens.)

PENDAKIS: It's my truck out there, lady. What's the problem?

NURSE: I just thought that you should know that a bunch of sailors are out in the parking lot celebrating Japan's defeat by letting all of your chickens free.

PENDAKIS: They have no right to do that!

TAKIS: It's not my fault, George. I locked the truck.

NIKOS: The same way you bet on Dead to Rights.

GEORGE: Those damn sailors! *(He runs out toward the parking lot.)*

TAKIS: *(Exiting)* Who's going to break in and steal a bunch of chickens?

(PENDAKIS follows his brothers out.)

NURSE: *(Shouts after them)* We got three of four trapped in the lobby downstairs.

(PENDAKIS rushes back in and hastily tucks some money into the bodice of the NURSE's uniform.)

PENDAKIS: Whatever you do, don't call the police. We can handle this ourselves.

(PENDAKIS rushes back out.)

NURSE: I can't take this. I've already called the police.

(The NURSE exits. MAX chuckles.)

ELAINE: You can always count on those two for something.

NIKOS: Hey, Max… Why don't you go help the boys? Give you some insight into the restaurant business.

ELAINE: Nicky, leave poor Max alone. He doesn't have to go if he doesn't want to.

MAX: No, it's alright. I need the exercise. The boys need my help. *(He exits.)*

NIKOS: That's right, Max. You go out there and play the good Samaritan.

ELAINE: Max doesn't deserve that.

NIKOS: That's right. I don't deserve anything. I certainly don't deserve to spend the rest of my life in this goddamn hospital.

(NIKOS *realizes that he is missing his cigar case that he carries in his shirt pocket.* MRS SATO *has it. She hands it to him.*)

NIKOS: *Sayonara...*

(MRS SATO *laughs.*)

NIKOS: She likes that. Sayonar... *(To* ELAINE*)* See, I know a little Japanese...Teriyaki.

ELAINE: Where did you learn your Japanese, Nicky?

NIKOS: *(To* MRS SATO*)* Hey, lady... Do you like chickens? Do..you..like...eatee...chickens... *(He flaps his arms and makes the sounds of a chicken.)* What's the matter with her?

(MRS SATO *stares at* NIKOS *and doesn't answer.*)

ELAINE: For God's sake Nicky she speaks better English than you do.

NIKOS: Then why doesn't she say something? Chickens?

ELAINE: Come on. Let's all go up together.

NIKOS: What the hell do we want to go upstairs for? They know where we are.

ELAINE: I believe that. I believe that all of New England knows where you are right at this moment.

EUNICE: There's nothing we can do upstairs... There's nothing we can do downstairs.

NIKOS: Nothing to do anywhere except go catch chickens.

EUNICE: Mrs Sato, I apologize for my husband. He sometimes gets carried away.

ELAINE: He ought to be carried away she means.

MRS SATO: I don't hurt anybody. I never hurt anybody in my whole life.

(From offstage we hear GEORGE's *voice.)*

GEORGE: *(Offstage)* Sailor take your foot off that chicken. It's still alive.

ELAINE: I knew there'd be a fight. *(She rushes off to her husband.)* George!

MRS SATO: Everything just go flooey.

*(*TAKIS *bursts into the room. We hear the sound of chickens. He skids across the floor. From offstage we can hear firecrackers going off. He makes a deliberate attempt to cheer up* NIKOS *and* EUNICE.*)*

TAKIS: *(To* MRS SATO*)* Did you see four chickens come this way? ...Some dumb shit's going around sticking firecrackers up their asses.

MRS SATO: *Omae ni nani mo ii ya shina.*

TAKIS: Thanks, lady. That helps a lot. *(He exits.)*

NIKOS: The world is filled with loonies...

(We hear the sounds of chickens clucking in the corridors of the hospital, and then we see a drunken SAILOR *enter the waiting room. He is not more than twenty or twenty-one, and he carries a small American flag in one hand and a white chicken feather in the other. He wears spectacles whose lenses have been smashed, and his right eye is bleeding profusely. He lets the feather go and it falls to the floor like a small bomb.)*

SAILOR: *(Singing)*
Old MacDonald had a farm.
eee-aye-eee-aye o,
And on that farm he had some chicks,
eee-aye-eee-aye o...

*(*GEORGE *enters, followed by* ELAINE. GEORGE *is brandishing a broomstick.)*

GEORGE: This is the sailor who let out the goddamn chickens. You're crazy for letting those chickens go.

SAILOR: I tripped over one of your chickens and broke my glasses.

GEORGE: *(Being held back by* NIKOS*)* You're going to pay seven cents a pound for those chickens.

NIKOS: *(Trying to help the* SAILOR*)* Eunie get a handkerchief.

SAILOR: I won't lose my eye? ...I don't want to lose my eye... Nurse!!!

GEORGE: *(Still in a rage)* Nurse!

SAILOR: I went through the whole war without a scratch and now look at me.

NIKOS: *(To the* SAILOR*)* Put your head back.

(The NURSE *has entered.)*

NURSE: Mister and Mrs Panayotopoulos?

NIKOS: There's someone here who needs your help.

NURSE: *(To* EUNICE*)* Doctor Carrus wants to see you both in his office right away.

EUNICE: Is it about Yannis? Is Yannis alright?

NURSE: You know where it is? On the third floor?

SAILOR: Owww!

(TAKIS re-enters.)

EUNICE: What did the doctors say? What did he say?

TAKIS: Where's Pendakis, he has the keys to the truck.

NIKOS: Tell us what he said!

NURSE: Go to him right away. He didn't say anything.

MRS SATO: *(Crossing to the* SAILOR*)* You want some bandages?

EUNICE: Nicky!

NURSE: Go sit down, Mrs Sato.

ELAINE: It's going to be good news, Eunie.

GEORGE: *(To* EUNICE*)* What do the doctors know.
They've made mistakes before.

NIKOS: We're going to take Yannis to Boston.

MRS SATO: I have lots of bandages.

NURSE; I told you to go sit down!

EUNICE: I know what he's going to say.

ELAINE: No, you don't, Eunie. Nobody knows what the
doctors are going to say.

SAILOR: What about my fucking eye?

NURSE: You watch your language, sailor.

NIKOS: *(To the* NURSE*)* Stop playing games with us!
And tell us what he said right now.

SAILOR: I didn't come home to die!

NURSE: For God's sake, sailor, their little boy died and
you're screaming about your friggin eye!

(The NURSE *steps back, realizing what she has said.*
PENDAKIS *enters, wiping his suit.)*

PENDAKIS: Well, the chicken war is over.

*(*GEORGE *looks at* PENDAKIS*.)*

SAILOR: My eye...

NURSE: I'll get the doctor. *(She exits.)*

NIKOS: *(Stepping toward* EUNICE*)* ...Eunie...

EUNICE: Keep away from me!

TAKIS: She's just a nurse. They don't tell the nurses
everything.

PENDAKIS: *(To* TAKIS*)* Soupa!

EUNICE: *(Helplessly)* Elaine.

SAILOR: My eye is killing me...

MRS SATO: It's a sad thing.

PENDAKIS: We're all here, Eunie...

(GEORGE *and* ELAINE *are getting* EUNICE's *possessions together.*)

PENDAKIS: ...We're all here, Eunie.

(EUNICE, ELAINE, PENDAKIS *and* GEORGE *exit slowly.* TAKIS *crosses to* NIKOS *and touches him on the shoulder.*)

TAKIS:...We gotta go upstairs, Nicky.

NIKOS: Don't touch me...just don't touch me... *(He crosses to leave and stops when he sees the* SAILOR) ...Did you see Max out there?

SAILOR: No.

NIKOS: *(With one of* MRS SATO's *rags)* You better not lose your eye...

(Hands him the rag) ...Here...Max!!!

*(*NIKOS *exits. Music begins.)*

TAKIS: *(After staring at the* SAILOR) ...Shut up!!! *(He exits.)*

SAILOR: *(To* MRS SATO) Hey, the war's over...I'm sorry.

(Lights fade. Music swells. End of scene)

Scene 4

(It is late morning of the day of Yannis' funeral. EUNICE *and* ELAINE *are dressed in black.* EUNICE *sits on the porch of her house and rocks back and forth in a rocking chair. With her is* ELAINE, *who sits off to one side with her hands folded in her lap. In the distance we can hear children playing. Perhaps a neighbor's radio, turned to a baseball game, can be heard.)*

EUNICE: We should have prepared him better.

ELAINE: Who, Eunie?

EUNICE: Philip.

ELAINE: You did everything you could. Nicky too.

EUNICE: No. We could have all prepared each other better.

ELAINE: There's nothing you can do. Nothing you can ever do.

EUNICE: Some people do. Not everybody keeps going on believing in miracles. Miracles are always something that happens to somebody else. They never seem to happen to us, do they? Like somebody is really going to go in there and raise Yannis up from the dead.

ELAINE: You think about Philip. You still have Philip. You hear me?

EUNICE: Poor kid. He's so filled with pills he doesn't know if he's coming or going.

ELAINE: As long as he's sleeping.

EUNICE: And his father out somewhere, running around like a wild man. He's out at the cemetery now, for what? He's only going to cause trouble out there too.

ELAINE: I'm sure he just has to be by himself for awhile.

EUNICE: And I can't believe what he did to Pendakis' chickens, taking all of them and tearing them apart like that.

ELAINE: That's Pendakis' worry, not yours. I'm sure at this point he doesn't care about those chickens.

EUNICE: Nobody's going to eat those chickens now.

ELAINE: Eunie, that's the nice thing about chickens. You can always buy more of them.

EUNICE: It's a sine to waste food like that. What with the starving people in China. You see how everything keeps going through my head at the same time? The stupid, the important...everything at once.

ELAINE: You should take a sedative...and lie down with your Philip.

EUNICE: Everything seems so important and so stupid at the same time. Did you ever listen to a baseball game and think that you would give your soul if only the Red Sox only won?

ELAINE: Me? I wait for Ted Williams to come back... and then I hope.

EUNICE: We should have prepared him better.

ELAINE: No one's ever prepared for that, Eunie. What about George and me? Do you think we could be prepared for that?

EUNICE: Some people are.

ELAINE: No. I don't believe it. It's like having the house, with a guest room, a room that is there, but somehow, you never go into it. Dark. Quiet halls.

EUNICE: *(Understanding)* ...The silent halls of death.

ELAINE: Or whatever.

EUNICE: Elaine, do you remember Sarah Haralampopolas' wedding about a month ago?

ELAINE: Her father changed his name to Jones.

EUNICE: Yes, well he couldn't accept his daughter's marriage, and he was reciting that line from *Love's Farewell*— "Since there is no help, come let us kiss and part..." I was the only one there who knew what he was quoting. And he couldn't get over it, that I knew it. There were all these other women around, but this man, he danced with me, and he was gorgeous—tall, white haired.

ELAINE: Not Nicky.

EUNICE: No, not Nicky.

(During the above, the three JANETAKIS *brothers enter...all are dressed for the funeral.)*

EUNICE: ...All afternoon we danced, and I recited to him all the poetry Mrs Vaughn had taught me...Nicky was so jealous, but I didn't care...I hadn't danced like that in ages.

GEORGE: *(Touching* EUNICE*)* It's time to go.

EUNICE: No.

GEORGE: Everybody's out there. We got a chauffeur. Everything...

TAKIS: Everybody's ready, Eunie...

EUNICE: Philip? Did somebody wake Philip?

PENDAKIS: Maybe it's better Philip sleeps, Eunie.

EUNICE: No...No... He won't forgive me... *(She begins to exit.)*

ELAINE: George, Nicky's been out there all morning. You go ahead and make certain everything's alright.

GEORGE: Alright...Pendakis...maybe you better...

PENDAKIS: Go with Charlie, George.

TAKIS: I'll drive...

*(*GEORGE *and* TAKIS *exit.)*

PENDAKIS: Elaine, you go with Zoe... Eunie, everything is going to be alright...alright.

(Music begins. Lights fade. End of scene)

Scene 5

(Bare stage representing Green Haven Cemetery. On stage is a PRIEST *adjusting his collar, and a young man,* HILLMAN O'CLAIR, *of 25 or so.* HILLMAN O'CLAIR *is dressed in an ill-fitting, wrinkled grey suit. He tugs uncomfortably at his tie. A plane passing overhead disturbs the relative calm.)*

PRIEST: Mister O'Clair, there is no one else with you?

O'CLAIR: I came by myself, Father.

PRIEST: I see.

O'CLAIR: Nobody.

PRIEST: There won't be any family then?

O'CLAIR: Wilbur was an orphan.

*(*MRS JAMES HILLIARD *enters the scene. She is a tall, red-haired woman, dressed in a dark purple dress. She wears a hat with a veil and carries a small bouquet of flowers.)*

MRS HILLIARD: Excuse me, Father, is this for Wilbur Ford?

PRIEST: Wilbur Ford? Yes. Yes, it is.

MRS HILLIARD: Oh good. I've been walking all over this place for the past half hour. These cemeteries are much larger than they look... *(She turns to* O'CLAIR*)* Are you the bill collector I talked to on the phone this morning?

O'CLAIR: Bill collector? Oh no, I'm just a friend of Wilbur's. That's all.

MRS HILLIARD: Just because I'm his landlady...ex-landlady...I don't know why I have to cope with all his debts...Are you the one that was in the army with him?

O'CLAIR: Who? Me? No. I tried to join, but they wouldn't take me.

MRS HILLIARD: A healthy young man like you 4F?

PRIEST: If we could please get started, Mrs...

MRS HILLIARD: Hilliard. Double "l".

PRIEST: Perhaps you and Mister O'Clair could stand along the side of the grave...

MRS HILLIARD: I know as soon as I get back the creditors will start crawling out of the woodwork.

PRIEST: He'll have to answer to a higher creditor now. *(He opens his bible and begins to read.)* ..."I said in mine heart concerning the estate of the sons of men, that God might manifest them, and that..."

(GEORGE and TAKIS both in mourning, rush in.)

TAKIS: Good thing I knew that short-cut. I told you we'd make it.

GEORGE: Some short-cut.

PRIEST: *(Continuing.)* "...they might see that they themselves are beats. For that which befalleth the sons of men befalleth-"

TAKIS: Where in the hell is everybody?

GEORGE: Father...one moment..wait!

PRIEST: Please, we have a service in progress here.

GEORGE: The rest of the family hasn't arrived yet, Father.

PRIEST: Family?

O'CLAIR: Wilbur had no family.

TAKIS: Excuse me, Father, but who is being buried here?

MRS HILLIARD: Who wants to know.

TAKIS: I want to know, that's who.

MRS HILLIARD: Didn't I tell you, Father, that the creditors wouldn't give us a chance to get him into the earth? *(To TAKIS)* What do you want? The gold from his teeth? Will that satisfy you vultures?

GEORGE: Vultures? We run the Chicken Coop, lady.

MRS HILLIARD: (*To* O'CLAIR) Even when you're dead, they don't leave well enough alone.

TAKIS: What's she talking about, Father? I'm looking for the Panayotopoulos funeral. There are supposed to be hundreds of people there.

PRIEST: Panayotopoulos funeral?

O'CLAIR: This is for Wilbur Ford.

TAKIS: Oh God…

GEORGE: You should listen to me, Takis, and do something right in your life for once.

TAKIS: It's got to be in another part of the cemetery, right?

PRIEST: This is the only funeral scheduled at Green Haven today.

TAKIS: Are you sure, Father?

MRS HILLIARD: Are you calling the Priest a liar?

TAKIS: Zoe said Green Haven, George. I swear it!!

GEORGE: Our old man is buried in Chelmsford. They're burying Yannis in Chelmsford!

O'CLAIR: That's all the way over on the other side of town.

GEORGE: (*To* HILLMAN O'CLAIR) What time is it?

O'CLAIR: Twelve thirty. What time was your funeral?

GEORGE: Twelve.

TAKIS: Noon, but we had car trouble.

MRS HILLIARD: Your funeral is probably all over by now.

GEORGE: I told you in the car…Chelmsford.

TAKIS: It's not fair. Zoe said Green Haven.

GEORGE: *(To* TAKIS*)* What's the sense of talking to you, Takis. It goes in one ear and out the other.

TAKIS: What are we going to tell Eunie.

PRIEST: Please, if you don't mind, I must get started. I have to be back at the church for a christening.

MRS HILLIARD: The Father's right. We might as well get it over with.

PRIEST: Sorry. I didn't mean it like that.

GEORGE: Come on, Takis.

TAKIS: I can't face her, George…Goddamn it…

GEORGE: Excuse him, Father…

TAKIS: Just go ahead without me, George.

GEORGE: What do you mean go ahead without you?

TAKIS: Leave me alone, George…

GEORGE: Give me the keys. *(He starts to exit.)*

TAKIS: It's too hot in the car, George. Who's being buried here, Father?

PRIEST: Wilbur Ford.

O'CLAIR: You might know him. He ran the dance studio on Keith Street.

GEORGE: For Christ Sakes, Takis.

PRIEST: It'll only take a moment once I get started.

MRS HILLIARD: I don't know any of your prayers or anything.

O'CLAIR: I wanted to serve in the army with him.

*(*TAKIS *removes his army hat.)*

TAKIS: *(To* GEORGE*)* What's a few more minutes to us?

PRIEST: May I begin?

GEORGE: *(Awkwardly)* Well...I used to go dancing on Keith Street.

PRIEST: *(Begins reading)* "I said in my heart—"

GEORGE: *(Removes his own hat)* Of course that was a long time ago.

PRIEST: "Concerning the estate of the sons of men, that God might manifest them, and that they might see that they themselves are beasts. For that which befalleth the sons of men befalleth beasts; even as one befalleth them: as one dieth, so dieth the other; yea, they have all one breath; so that a man hath no pre-eminence above a beast; for all is vanity. All go unto one place; all are of the dust, and all turn to dust again."

(The PRIEST *quickly exits. The music swells.* MRS HILLIARD *exits.* O'CLAIR *shakes hands with* TAKIS *and then she exits. The two brothers are left alone staring at the grave. Lights fade to black. End of scene.)*

Scene 6

(Lights fade up. We are at RITA's *farmhouse. It is early morning several days after the funeral.* MAX *is knocking at the door. A dog is barking in the front yard.)*

GEORGE: Pendakis, what's his car doing out here?!!!

PENDAKIS: Skamos, George!!

MAX: *(Whispering)* Pendakis!

PENDAKIS: Knock on the door, Max. It's the first step in the chicken business. Can't open a restaurant without food, Max.

GEORGE: *(Voice)* What's his car doing out here?

PENDAKIS: *(To* GEORGE*)* Skamos!

MAX: Pendakis, I think she's coming.

(RITA *emerges from her bedroom and is in the process of tightening her robe.*)

RITA: Can't a woman get some sleep?

MAX: Move your tuchis, Pendakis.

RITA: Who is it?

PENDAKIS: Come on, Rita. Open up.

(RITA *glances backward toward the bedroom.*)

RITA: So the thief is here. What do you want to steal this time?

PENDAKIS: We brought the money we owe you.

RITA: Really? Yeah, after I had to threaten to send the cops after you.

PENDAKIS: The cops in this town are all our friends, right George?

GEORGE: Hey…

RITA: Yeah, you think you and your brothers know everybody and you think the Foscolos don't.

MAX: Pendakis, maybe we should come back another time.

PENDAKIS: It's alright, Max.

RITA: Who's out there with you?

PENDAKIS: Somebody George and I want you to meet, Rita.

RITA: *(Reluctantly)* Alright, come in.

MAX: *(Apologetically)* They said you'd be up.

PENDAKIS: Rita, this is Max Abrahamson, the new owner of the Chicken Coop…Max, Rita, Foscolo, Queen of the Chicken Breeders… We thought you should get acquainted since you'll be doing business together…Max, pay the lady…

(MAX *hands her an envelope.*)

MAX: *(Removing his hat)* I'm very pleased to meet you. I've heard a lot about you.

RITA: I bet.

MAX: Good things.

RITA: They're all thieves top to bottom. When you shake hands with them, you have to count your fingers.

PENDAKIS: Not going to ask us to sit down, Rita?

(PENDAKIS *crosses and sits in* RITA's *rocking chair.*)

RITA: Please, Pendakis. I have to get breakfast for my children... Why didn't you phone before coming over?

PENDAKIS: You're always here.

RITA: That's right. Where would I go, huh?

(MAX *pays for chickens, counts out some change to add to the bills.*)

MAX: Forty-two, eighty.

RITA: If you want more chickens, see me later in the week. I'm not awake now.

PENDAKIS: Not even going to offer Max a cup of coffee, Rita?

RITA: Coffee?

MAX: Please don't go to any trouble on my account.

PENDAKIS: It's no trouble, Max.

(MAX *stands up.*)

MAX: We'll come back later in the week.

PENDAKIS: Where's Nicky, Rita?

(MAX *sits down again.*)

RITA: I don't know what you're talking about.

PENDAKIS: Don't give me that, Rita. We saw his car out back.

RITA: Leave him alone, huh.

PENDAKIS: *(Loudly)* You want me to go in there and get him?

RITA: That's my bedroom back there. It's not Grand Central Station. You stay out of it.

*(*NIKOS *has entered dressed in his undershirt, shorts and socks.)*

RITA: Would you like some coffee, Max?

MAX: That would be very nice, thank you.

NIKOS: You sons of bitches! What in the hell are you doing here?

PENDAKIS: Get dressed, Nicky.

NIKOS: That's what you think. *(Swears in Greek)*

RITA: So you're going into the restaurant business, huh, Max?

MAX: Yes.

RITA: You'll love every minute of it.

NIKOS: I'm entitled to a life of my own. I won't sit around and just wait to die like you two and Takis. I don't own my soul to you and the restaurant business, or no one. Now get the hell out of here before I throw you out.

PENDAKIS: Eunie needs you now.

NIKOS: She knows I'm here?

PENDAKIS: Of course not.

NIKOS: Who knows I'm here? Zoe? *(To* GEORGE*)* Elaine know I'm here? What? is it plastered all over the newspapers or what? *(Pointing to* MAX*)* And what did you bring him here for? You want me to be paying blackmail for the rest of my life?

PENDAKIS: Are you crazy? Max isn't going to tell anybody. Are you, Max?

NIKOS: No? I know how those Jews do business. Don't tell me...

PENDAKIS: Rita, get his clothes.

RITA: One minute ago I was Queen of the Chickens. Now you treat me like a servant.

(RITA *crosses into the bedroom.*)

MAX: *(Apologetically)* I should know you were going to be here?

PENDAKIS: I wanted Max to meet Rita.

NIKOS: Ah, great! That's wonderful. Kill two birds with one stone, is that it?

PENDAKIS: You being at home right now.

NIKOS: Don't tell me where I belong. I don't tell you where to stick you oar.

PENDAKIS: Get dressed or I'll take you home like that.

NIKOS: *(Violently)* AGAMISSU!!!

PENDAKIS: *(Stands up)* I'll break your ass!

(RITA *returns and tosses* NIKOS' *clothes on the table.*)

RITA: I don't want any fighting in here.

NIKOS: What do I want to go home for? So I can breed more kids to throw into the ground? No, thank you. I live for me now, that's all. I'm not going to wake up at the end of my life and go through a long list of missed opportunities like Takis and the racing form... all the races he should have bet on... No, sir, I live for me now...that's all... I'll never forgive you for this,

Pendakis. I swear to God. Barging in here like this...
Bringing him here with you... I'll never forgive you...

PENDAKIS: Rita, Max needs thirty-five chickens by next Monday... You take care of him, Rita.

RITA: We'll see, Pendakis. I want you out of here before my chickens wake up.

PENDAKIS: It's cash on the barrel-head, Max.

MAX: We can make it a standing order, yes? ...Mondays?

(NIKOS *and* PENDAKIS *are on opposite sides of the table.*)

PENDAKIS: *(Looking at* NIKOS*)* And one more thing, Rita. I don't want Nicky ever to step foot in this house again. You understand?

(NIKOS *gives out a roar, and leaps across the table at* PENDAKIS. PENDAKIS *grabs* NIKOS *and pulls him to the floor.* NIKOS' *pants have fallen about his ankles.*)

RITA: Max, do something!

MAX: *(Sits calmly)* Don't pay any attention to them! They do that all the time.

(NIKOS *gets up and approaches* PENDAKIS *ready to punch him.*)

PENDAKIS: Go ahead!

(NIKOS *can't. His hands go down.* PENDAKIS *slaps* NIKOS *then kisses him to forgive him.*)

MAX: They do that all the time, too.

PENDAKIS: *(Abruptly)* Max, you go with George. I'll take Nikos. Come on!

RITA: *(Handing* NIKOS *his jacket)* ...Nikos...

(RITA *and* NIKOS *look at one another.* NIKOS *exits.*)

GEORGE: *(Following his brothers out)* Max, don't forget about the eggs.

MAX: Eggs?

RITA: Eggs too?

(GEORGE *exits. Music begins.)*

MAX: I'm learning… It's a nice place you got here…
cozy. *(He exits.)*

RITA: Yeah…cozy…

(Lights fade to black. Music swells. End of scene.)

Scene 7

*(Lights fade up. It is late afternoon, approximately
two months after the funeral. We are in the attic of the*
PANAYOTOPOULOS *house.* EUNICE *has two drawers of
clothes. She is separating* YANNIS' *things. She takes out a
toy trunk.* NIKOS *enters.)*

NIKOS: Maybe Philip wants some of this stuff.

EUNICE: He doesn't.

NIKOS: How do you know?

EUNICE: Because I asked him. That's why. How do you
think I know?

NIKOS: Alright. I just asked. That's all.

EUNICE: Maybe if you talked with him, maybe you
would know too.

NIKOS: I said alright, didn't I? No need to make a case
out of it.

EUNICE: Nikos, just leave me alone.

NIKOS: *(Quietly)* I could hear you rummaging around
in here. I just came up to see what you were doing.

EUNICE: Well now you know. I wanted to look at some
of Yannis' things, that's all. Is there a crime in that?

NIKOS: Should I get a match and set fire to it?

EUNICE: Oh you would like that, wouldn't you?

NIKOS: Like what?

EUNICE: To pretend we never had Yannis. Just pick up where we left off with Philip, pretending that Yannis never existed.

NIKOS: It's a shame people can't do that. It would make life a lot easier all the way around.

EUNICE: Even if I had the choice, I wouldn't.

NIKOS: Well, you ain't got the choice. You're talking nonsense as usual.

EUNICE: Everything is nonsense to you.

NIKOS: Yea, everything that Mrs Vaughn or Van or whatever her goddamn names was put into your head was, that's for sure.

EUNICE: You don't know anything about it and you never will.

NIKOS: No?

EUNICE: You don't know anything that goes through my head.

NIKOS: No?

EUNICE: No.

NIKOS: Forgive me. I forget sometimes that everybody on the Janetakis side of the family is a flaming genius.

EUNICE: You're jealous. That's all.

NIKOS: No, I'm not jealous… These people, they invented horse racing and built the finest restaurant this side of bankruptcy… (He hold his hands out with his fingers spread apart.) …You see this?

EUNICE: What's that?

NIKOS: That's the combined I Q of your whole family.

EUNICE: What do you care? You don't care about anybody.

NIKOS: I care about you. I care about Philip.

EUNICE: You never cared.

NIKOS: When I say I care it means I care. Now you stop it. When I say I care it means I care.

EUNICE: Keep away from me.

NIKOS: Don't you ever say I don't care.

EUNICE: *(Taunting him)* ...You don't care..you don't care... You don't care...

(NIKOS *slaps her, flailing at her back and shoulders.*)

NIKOS: Goddammit, Eunie, what the hell are you doing to me?

EUNICE: Is that the only way you can feel something?

NIKOS: It's the only way I can get to you.

EUNICE: Nothing will ever get to me again.

NIKOS: Come on, for Christ sakes, Eunie, even World War II, it comes to an end. You throw the dead into the ditch and you walk away.

EUNICE: Not me.

NIKOS: Let me finish goddammit...will you let me finish for once... You walk away as much as you can walk away...because the dead and the living are all mixed up together... What if we raised Yanni up and he got killed in the war like a million of other people? Does his life make any more sense? Is it any more meaningful?

EUNICE: I don't want to talk with you about it.

NIKOS: Well you better talk to somebody about it.

EUNICE: Why don't you slap me again?

NIKOS: I would if I thought it would help. I would.

EUNICE: Nothing you do helps.

NIKOS: I did everything I could do. What the hell more could I do?

EUNICE: It wasn't enough.

NIKOS: *(A cry)* It's never enough...I can't play God. I can't stop people from dying.

EUNICE: Nobody asked you play God, Nicky. *(She slaps him hard many times.)* ...Just be my husband, that's all... Just be my husband... Where were you, Nicky? What happened to you? Where did you go? Where are you now? Are you here? ...Are you here? ...God... *(She catches herself.)*

NIKOS: I don't know...I don't know... I'll tell you one thing I do know. Our lives go on. That's all...it's not much...but that's all I know.

EUNICE: Well, I know better.

NIKOS: You know better.

EUNICE: I know what I need... What am I supposed to do, Nicky when you're out running around the city like a madman? When I'm comforting Philip, who's comforting me?

NIKOS: What the hell are you talking about? Your goddamn bothers and their wives are running around this house like Coxie's Army, for Christ sakes...I have to parachute in to get a word in edge wise.

EUNICE: A brother is not a husband, Nicky. There's nothing in this house that talks to me anymore. Nothing. Sometimes I just want to be held, Nicky. Who is supposed to know that better than you? Our family, friends, strangers? They come into our house, they walk up and down our stairs, they pace back and forth over our carpets, they sit in our chairs with long faces, they want to say something but there is nothing to say, so what do they do, they don't say anything at all, or they stare at me like I'm a freak. My son has died and I'm a freak for it...because something abnormal has happened, and someone or something is to blame.

NIKOS: There is no one to blame...no one to blame... Why can't you understand that? There's no one to blame.

EUNICE: *(Takes NIKOS' face in her hands)* Nicky, look at me... Look at me! I feel like something has sliced me open and pulled back my skin...

NIKOS: For Christ sakes, stop it Eunie, stop it.

EUNICE: Look at me...I have nothing to protect myself with anymore.

NIKOS: *(Embracing EUNICE)* Then we protect each other...then we protect each other...

EUNICE: I want to sell the house, Nicky...

NIKOS: We'll see...we'll see...

EUNICE: No... We have to. I won't live here anymore.

NIKOS: If we have to, we have to.

EUNICE: I mean it, Nicky.

NIKOS: Alright... I said alright... If that's what you want, we sell the house... It's alright... Now that Max has bought the restaurant, maybe he wants a house to live in... It's certainly a better value than the Chicken Coop... Anyway, there's going to be tons of G Is looking for places.

PHILIP: *(Offstage)* Mama...Mama...Mama...

(PHILIP rushes into the room. He still wears the neck brace.)

NIKOS: How many times do I have to tell you not to run with that neck brace on?

PHILIP: Mama! I saw Yannis. I saw Yannis.

NIKOS: What the hell you mean you saw Yannis?

PHILIP: I saw him skating right in front of the house.

NIKOS: What are you talking about? Running here...

EUNICE: Nicky, please. *(To* PHILIP*)* O K, now Philip. Just take a deep breath. Now exactly where did you see Yannis?

PHILIP: On the sidewalk in front of the house. Just a few minutes ago. I think he's still there... Cross my heart and hope to die....stick a needle in my eye...I saw him I really did.

NIKOS: O K. We believe you. You saw Yannis.

EUNICE: Come to the window and show us.

*(*PHILIP *points, but he will not go to the window.)*

PHILIP: Right down there... I saw him... He past right by...waving at me...

EUNICE: Are you sure it was Yannis?

PHILIP: No, Mamma, I saw him.

NIKOS: Whose skates did he have on?

EUNICE: Is it possible that you just saw somebody who looked like him?

PHILIP: But he waved at me.

EUNICE: I know darling, but sometimes under certain conditions...

PHILIP: Do you think I saw a ghost, Mama? Do you think I saw Yannis' ghost?

EUNICE: How long ago did it happen, Philip? Tell me exactly.

PHILIP: Just a few minutes ago. He waved at me, Mama.

EUNICE: Keep calm, Philip. We must be very quiet. *(She crosses away from the window toward the door.)*

NIKOS: Where are you going?

EUNICE: I want to see if Yannis' skates are still in the garage.

PHILIP: I'll go with you.

EUNICE: No. You stay here with your father. I'll be right back.

NIKOS: Stay here with me. Let your mama go check.

(EUNICE *goes downstairs.*)

PHILIP: Are ghosts dangerous?

NIKOS: Well, you never know.

PHILIP: *(Playing with toys in the trunk)* In Abbot and Costello movies they're funny.

NIKOS: Everything's funny in an Abbot and Costello movie. Even the airplane crashes.

PHILIP: Yannis' ghost wouldn't be dangerous, would he?

NIKOS: Well, I don't think so. Not to us anyway... Maybe some doctors he might want to get back at.

PHILIP: Where do you think he was going skating by like that?

NIKOS: Probably to the Ballroom at Saint Patrick's Cathedral. That's where all the ghosts skate to these days... They have a great big roller rink and...

PHILIP: I know that joke.

NIKOS: Who's telling you jokes like that? Johnny Vernalis?

PHILIP: Uncle Takis told me.

NIKOS: Figures.

PHILIP: I think it's very funny.

NIKOS: You do, huh? Well I don't want you going around repeating that joke to people. You're not old enough to be telling those kid jokes.

PHILIP: For your information, I'm going to be thirteen soon.

NIKOS: Yeah...well for your information I didn't know jokes like that until I was twice your age and even then I didn't understand half of them.

PHILIP: Well, I'll explain them to you if you want.

NIKOS: Oh you will, will you.

(PHILIP *is looking in a scrapbook.* NIKOS *finds an old record player.*)

NIKOS: Bet you never saw this before.

PHILIP: Pop?

NIKOS: What?

PHILIP: What's this? (*He holds a dance card in his hand.*)

NIKOS: You don't know what this is? See, wise guy, you don't know everything.

PHILIP: I just asked. How am I going to learn if I don't ask questions?

NIKOS: (*Holding the card*) This is a dance card from your mother's graduation. You see the list of names on it? A lot of them are dead now, but this is a list of all the men she danced with on her graduation night.

PHILIP: Why?

NIKOS: What do you mean "why?"

PHILIP: Couldn't she remember who she was going to dance with?

NIKOS: Of course she could remember...that's the way they did those things.

PHILIP: How come I don't see your name on it?

NIKOS: Cause I didn't know her then.

PHILIP: Did you and Mama ever dance again?

NIKOS: Of course we danced together. I was quite a dancer in my day.

PHILIP: Sure.

NIKOS: Gliding around the ballroom in a tux.

PHILIP: Yuk.

NIKOS: What the hell do you know? Kid's today don't know nothing about dancing. They just do this crazy stuff that looks as if their arms and legs are falling off.

PHILIP: For your information, it's called Jitterbugging.

NIKOS: Yeah…well for your information it looks like a bunch of sh…

(NIKOS *holds back.* PHILIP *continues to play with the toy chest.*)

NIKOS: Come here. Give me this *(The dance card)* …Look take this card and when your mama comes upstairs tell her that I've signed up for the next dance. *(He signs the card.)*

PHILIP: What for?

NIKOS: What do you mean what for? Because I told you to. That's what for… For your mama, alright… Because it'll bring back good memories to her. Isn't that reason enough?

PHILIP: Someday I'm going to get old and make you do stupid things.

NIKOS: I hope so.

PHILIP: Do you really think Yannis' skates are gone?

NIKOS: If they were gone, she'd be shouting up the stairs by now.

PHILIP: But I saw him. I really did.

NIKOS: Alright. You saw him. So don't make such a big thing about it. It just means that the next time he comes by, we'll be ready for him. Go on... I can hear your mother.

PHILIP: No. Maybe it's a ghost.

NIKOS: There are no ghosts. Only ghosts up here. (*Points to his head*)

PHILIP: I'm not crazy.

NIKOS: I don't say you're crazy. I see ghosts too...all the time... Now go...

PHILIP: I'm scared.

NIKOS: There's nothing to be scared of. It's all family.

PHILIP: That's what I'm scared of.

NIKOS: Do you really want me to break your neck? Now go...

(*EUNICE re-enters.*)

PHILIP: Mama?

EUNICE: Everything's alright, Philip.

PHILIP: Did you find the skates?

EUNICE: They're still in the garage. They haven't been moved.

(*PHILIP hands her the dance card.*)

EUNICE: What's this?

PHILIP: Pop says he wants the next dance. You see, he signed his name on it.

EUNICE: It's from my graduation dance. Where did you get it?

NIKOS: He found it in one of the scrapbooks.

(*PHILIP sits cross-legged in the middle of the floor.*)

EUNICE: Philip, get off the floor. What are you sitting on the floor for?

PHILIP: Pop said if you and him danced together I could watch.

NIKOS: What! *(To* EUNICE*)* He doesn't believe that his old man was a great dancer.

EUNICE: No?

NIKOS: No. kids nowadays don't believe anything unless you show them.

EUNICE: Well, you tell your father to put away his cigar and we'll see.

PHILIP: Well, put away your cigar and we'll see.

NIKOS: Move back. You can't sit in the middle of the ballroom, stupid.

*(*NIKOS *moves some chairs out of the way. He motions for* PHILIP *to turn on the record player. The music begins.* EUNICE *takes off her apron.* NIKOS *takes his wife in his arms and begin a slow dance.)*

PHILIP: I saw a ghost, didn't I, Mama?

EUNICE: Yes, dear. I saw him too.

(Music ends. NIKOS *and* EUNICE *stop dancing. Lights out.)*

(Curtain)

END OF PLAY

www.ingramcontent.com/pod-product-compliance
Lightning Source LLC
Chambersburg PA
CBHW052153090426
42741CB00010B/2255